Golf at the Top with Steve Williams

Golf at the Top with Steve Williams

Tips & Techniques
from the Caddy to
Raymond Floyd,
Greg Norman &
Tiger Woods

Steve Williams & Hugh de Lacy

Foreword by TIGER WOODS

Ulysses Press

Published by: Ulysses Press
P.O. Box 3440
Berkeley, CA 94703
www.ulyssespress.com

ISBN 1-56975-527-2
Library of Congress Control Number 2005908370

Printed in Canada by Transcontinental Printing

10 9 8 7 6 5 4 3

Cover design: Robles-Aragón
Cover photograph: © Harry How/Gettyimages.com
Interior design: Leslie Henriques
Editorial and production: Amy Hough, Matt Orendorff,
   Kathryn Brooks
Index: Sayre Van Young

Distributed by Publishers Group West

Table of Contents

Foreword   7

1 Ten feet tall and bulletproof   9

2 Garbage in, garbage out   21

3 Packaging the messages   32

4 The art of concentration   42

5 The snowball effect   52

6 The great triumvirate: desire, concentration
  and goal-setting   62

7 Goals—the long and short of it   75

8 Affirmations—schooling the subconscious   90

9 Visualization, imagination and creativity   99

10 Relaxation techniques   110

11 Anchoring, temperament and the
   meaning of "feel"   121

12 The paradox of the peak experience   131

13 Harnessing fear, managing pain   143

14 Gamesmanship   153

15 Five hot tips for the handicap player   160

16 Caddying in the zone   166

Index   178

Acknowledgments   185

About the Authors   187

Foreword

Among the thousands of golf books that have been published, few have dared to tackle the way the golfing mind works, let alone offer a simple and practical blueprint for training it. Steve Williams and Hugh de Lacy have set out to fill that gap with *Golf at the Top with Steve Williams*.

I think they've succeeded brilliantly.

Since inviting Stevie to join my team in 1999, I've come to appreciate the vast store of golfing wisdom and experience he has amassed in his 25 years on the professional tour. As the most successful caddy in the history of the game, with more than 100 tournament wins to his credit, Stevie has set the standard by which the modern professional caddy is judged.

As you will see from the anecdotes throughout this book, Stevie and my relationship has long since surpassed the purely professional. We have become close friends, and our friendship is based on that most important of ingredients: mutual respect.

In *Golf at the Top with Steve Williams*, Stevie and Hugh show that any golfer, whatever their experience, skills and ambition, can set themselves on a path of rapid improvement in the game by adopting the simple disciplines of mind-training.

Golf needs this book. I congratulate Stevie and Hugh on producing it, and recommend it to anyone who wants to explore their true and full potential as a golfer.

—Tiger Woods

1

Ten Feet Tall and Bulletproof

Competitive golf is played mainly on a five-and-a-half inch course—the space between your ears.

—Bobby Jones

We hadn't been together long, the fresh-faced sophomore golfing sensation from middle America, and me, the globetrotting veteran caddy from where-in-the-world-is New Zealand. It had been barely a month since I had gotten the call, out of the blue, to carry the bag of the youngest ever Masters winner, 12 years my junior and the hottest golfer on the planet.

I was honored that Tiger Woods chose me to carry his bag for him. Despite my qualification of over 60 wins in professional golf tournaments and the fact that pros who've hired me to carry their bags have ended up winning with greater consistency, Tiger Woods, barely 23 years old and already hailed as the greatest golfer since Jack Nicklaus, had his pick of any professional caddy in the world.

And there wasn't one of them who wouldn't have leapt at the job.

At the time Tiger called in early 1999, I hadn't seen a single winter in 20 years of carrying the bag for some of the world's best golfers, so a comfortable retirement back home in the South Pacific was beginning to beckon. I had already achieved and earned more than I had ever hoped to when I first launched myself into a globetrotting career all those years earlier. I'd been with my current employer, Raymond Floyd, for 11 years, and had helped the seemingly ageless American become the only person to win tournaments on both the PGA and Seniors (Champions) Tours in the same year (1992). Although Floyd was still going strong in his late fifties, I was starting to think of bringing the curtain down on the endless summer of golf.

But all thoughts of retirement quickly evaporated when I took Tiger's call.

Tiger had recently split with Mike "Fluff" Cowan, the colorful and media-savvy old-timer who had guided him through the transition from gifted amateur to money-spinning professional. He had come of age under Cowan's guardianship, but now his need was for a caddy who could stimulate and extend him, as well as plot strategies and read the fairways and traps on the world's most lucrative tournament circuits.

It was Tiger's coach, Claude "Butch" Harmon, who first got in touch with me. Harmon, the son of 1948 Masters winner Claude Harmon senior, caught up with me on March 5, 1999, at the Doral-Ryder Open in Miami, Florida, where I was once again looping for Raymond Floyd. Tiger Woods himself followed up Harmon's initial contact by way of a 20-minute telephone conversation on the following day, Saturday.

Within 24 hours we had an agreement.

We got together for our first practice session two weeks later, and two days after that we lined up for our first tournament, the Bay Hill Invitational in Orlando, Florida.

It was a pretty inauspicious start to our partnership, Tiger managing only a 74 in the first round and nearly missing the cut. He did better in our next outing, the Players Championship, finishing 10th.

Here we were, in just our fourth tournament together—the 1999 Hilton Head Classic at the Harbour Town Golf Club in South Carolina. We'd reached the 15th hole, a 575-yard beast of a par five with a fairway barely 20 yards wide and hemmed in by huge trees on both sides. To top it off, the hole was defended against a direct second shot by a left-hand dogleg, a water hazard and a stockade of giant pines.

I had been to Hilton Head a dozen times before, with both Floyd and another long-time boss (eight years), Australia's "Great White Shark" Greg Norman. I had seen Harbour Town's 15th wreck the scorecards of some of the best professionals in the game, though they treated it with due caution and took the long way round the dogleg.

But that was not the way of Tiger Woods, the lanky young man with the whippy swing who'd burst onto the professional scene after becoming the first player to win the United States Amateur Championship three years in a row. He handled Harbour Town's 15th differently. He started out with a drive that traveled a full 300 yards down the center of that throttling fairway. Then, after checking the yardages with me, he selected the four iron and lofted the ball high over the encroaching trees, the water hazard and the protective pines. It traveled 240 yards and came up just short of the green, out of our sight.

Then he did it again in each of the following three rounds.

It hardly mattered to me that we finished only 18th in that tournament. I was exhilarated by Tiger's approach to the game, a marriage of sublime skills with intense competitiveness and seemingly unshakable self-confidence. His treatment of the murderous 15th at Hilton Head exemplified it. He wasn't throwing caution to the wind when he opted to take the short cut to the hole over the trees and across the corner of the dogleg. Instead, using the yardages I had compiled over years of surveying the course in advance and the direction I prescribed to the invisible green, Tiger precisely assessed both the height and the distance he could extract from his four iron.

Then he executed the shot with machine-like accuracy.

More significantly, in my opinion, Tiger was driven to attempt such a shot by the knowledge that no one else in the field would trust themselves to do so, and he could accordingly grab a one-shot advantage by making it himself. The intensity of his desire to win drove him to make the shot; he was confident in his ability to pull it off, and he craved the competitive advantage it would give him.

This was the attitude that captivated me that day on the 15th at Harbour Town: the intensity of the will to win expressed through his craft by this unshakably modest and polite young man who had the golfing world at his feet.

I remain captivated by his attitude today.

Inspiration

Tiger Woods wasn't the first professional golfer whose sublime skills enthralled me, convincing me that there was a way I could make an even greater contribution to the game than by swinging the clubs myself. The person who set me on the path to a caddying career was the Australian five-time British Open winner, Peter Thomson.

It happened in 1976, a couple of months after Tiger Woods was born, at a time when I was training to become a professional golfer myself.

I dreamt of becoming a professional golfer or an international rugby player. I wanted to be an All Black—a member of the legendary New Zealand team that for more than a century has made the tiny South Pacific country synonymous with the full-body-contact sport of rugby union football.

In 1976, at the age of 13, I was appointed captain of the New Zealand under-15 schoolboys' rugby team for a match against Australia, playing in the front row of the scrum where the physical contact is at its most intense. I was already nearly six feet tall and powerfully built, and in the normal course of events, I could have graduated through the ranks to become a full All Black by my early twenties. I could have been part of a sport, still doggedly amateur in those days, that has shaped my native country's egalitarian character more than any other. Perhaps I could have been there wearing the black jersey that day in 1987 when New Zealand beat France in the final to win the inaugural Rugby World Cup.

But while rugby pulled me in one direction, golf pulled me in another. My home town of Paraparaumu, which is 50 miles north of the capital city of Wellington, helped to influence my decision because it was the site of the best links-style golf course in the country.

The Paraparaumu Golf Club features a classic course that looks like it has been uprooted from golf's birthplace on the coasts of Scotland and transplanted to the other side of the world. It's set among rolling dunes and features well-drained fairways, fast greens, merciless rough and harrowing bunkers. Rated by *Golf* magazine among the 100 best courses in the world, it was designed in 1949 by former Australian Open champion Alex Russell. Thereafter it rapidly became the focal point of the dormitory and retirement village of Paraparaumu, which has since grown into a substantial town. The course was, and remains, the town's focal point, and I could no more ignore its magnetism than an actor could ignore Hollywood.

However, it wasn't Paraparaumu and my relative success as a golfer that turned me away from rugby (though I was already down to a handicap of two by the time I was 13 years old). Instead it was my father, John Williams, who brought me and Peter Thomson together, thereby inadvertently launching me, his headstrong son, on a caddying career.

My father had been a leading amateur in the 1950s and '60s, a time when Thomson was cutting his teeth on the Australian and New Zealand circuits. He and Peter Thomson had played against each other frequently, and in the process developed a close and lasting friendship. Their relationship survived when Thomson turned professional after leading home the amateur field in the 1948 Australian Open. Thomson quickly graduated to the professional ranks on the English and European circuits, becoming the first player of the modern era to win the British Open three years in a row (1954–56) and to finish either first or second seven years in a row (1952–58). His last British Open win was in 1965.

Thomson was one of the game's great thinkers, both on and off the course. He was clever, plotting in advance the way he would tackle a given course, and he analyzed each shot before stepping up to play it. He was a links specialist, by far preferring hard and fast-running courses which demanded a shot tailored to every situation. He admired the well-watered tracks in the United States that were breeding grounds for the upcoming generation of big-hitting Americans, of whom Tiger Woods would become the most revered.

Off the course Thomson applied his analytical mind to politics, among other things— he contemplated a political career back in Australia, but instead gave momentum to golf's invasion of the East by designing and building courses throughout Asia. Only later did the big money of the Seniors Tour draw him to the United States, where in 1985, he had by far the most lucrative year of his career, winning $350,000. That was the year he showed he'd finally mastered American-style golf courses by winning no fewer than nine Seniors tournaments, a feat only equaled since by Hale Irwin in 1997.

By the time Thomson lined up for the 1976 New Zealand Open at Heretaunga, Lower Hutt, with me as his caddy, it had been 11 years since his fifth and final British Open win. But his vision of golf as a mind game was as sharp as ever.

The way Thomson seemed to wrestle as much with his own mental approach to the game—distinct from the purely physical challenge of belting the ball down the fairway to the green and nudging it into the cup—captured my imagination. It was as if Thomson had introduced a new and separate element of the game to me.

Under Thomson's influence I found myself examining the big underlying questions of the game, such as the relationship between the player, the club and the stationary ball, and how that dictates the outcome of the stroke. Given that the club and the ball are inanimate objects, Thomson told me, the key performance factor is how the player's mind relates to them during the second or so it takes to execute the stroke. That got me wondering what sort of training processes the player had to put his mind through to ensure the optimum geometry of clubhead on ball during the millisecond of impact.

To a kid who had gleefully chased the little white ball round the Paraparaumu links (just over the hill from Heretaunga), always seeing the ball as the object of focus, Thomson's approach was mind-blowing.

Thomson took the obligation to perform entirely off the ball, the club and the swing, and put it where it belonged: in the mind of the player. What the ball did, I learned, was inescapably a function of what the mind was doing at the time of the impact of the club on the ball. Practice was not a matter of training the ball, the club or the swing to behave as desired, so much as training the mind to exert the greatest possible control over the ball's behavior through the agencies of the swing and the club.

That being the case, Thomson suggested to me during those mind-boggling rounds on the picturesque Heretaunga course, the caddy's role was vastly more important than just carting the player's bag from shot to shot. Teamed up with the right player, the caddy had the potential to be as indispensable a part of the player's equipment as his ball and clubs: the caddy had to be part strategist, part psychologist, part mathematician, as well as a walking encyclopedia of the course and its quirks.

There was one final lesson Thomson taught me as a teenager.

At the 1976 New Zealand Open, Thomson showed the still-solid form he would shortly begin to demonstrate on the U.S. Seniors Tour. He finished third, much to my delight, because my local knowledge helped get him there. And though his prize money was notably modest by British Open standards, at the end of the tournament Thomson gave me $150 cash, his golf bag and a stack of practice balls.

At the time this was untold wealth to me—I had been supplementing the 50-cents-a-week pocket money I got from my parents by fishing golf balls out of water hazards at my home course of Paraparaumu. It made my newly discovered vision of the caddy's role not just mentally alluring, not just magnetically adventurous—all that travel, all those exciting people, all those exotic places—but financially attractive as well. It offered me the world with a pay packet, something I could never have gotten banging heads in a rugby scrimmage on an amateur's measly daily allowance.

I definitely had aspirations to be a golf pro when I was younger. But the very first time I caddied, I discovered I had a knack for it. I could see school—high school or pro school—was no good for me. I just wanted to be a caddy.

Enlightened Truancy

Of course my parents weren't wildly happy about their eldest son's new-found fixation. Neither was my school, nor the rugby coach who was expecting me to eventually don the hallowed All Black jersey.

But I was like a colt with the bit between its teeth, and there wasn't a lot any of them could do about it. I knew I wouldn't get far in the professional golfing world on Peter Thomson's golf bag and $150, so without telling my parents, I ditched school, lied about my age (not for the last time) and got a job in a butcher's shop to earn money to travel.

My Kapiti High School truancy officer pretty soon discovered what was going on, and I found myself suspended—which amounted to being punished by allowing me to do exactly what I was doing anyway. And when I didn't go back to school at the end of my suspension, they suspended me again, which was even better. I was suspended until I turned 15, when it became legal for me to quit school altogether.

With my earnings from the butcher's shop, I paid my way around the country's few professional tournaments. These included the 1977 Air New Zealand Open in Auckland, where I ran into a couple of professional American caddies who fed my hunger to get onto the world professional golf circuit. Yes, they assured me, there was excitement, travel and money to be had from caddying.

All I had to do was be good enough.

Later, my father got a catch-up call from Peter Thomson, asking if I could carry his bags in the upcoming Australian Open. I like to think I had made almost as big an impression on Thomson as the old pro had made on me. My parents were understandably perturbed at the prospect of their scholastically wayward son taking up a temporary job with at-best-uncertain prospects in a foreign country. But Thomson promised them he'd look after me, and try to land me a professional golf apprenticeship over there. Whatever reservations they had about Thomson's offer, my parents resigned themselves to the reality that there was no stopping me anyway.

So with a wave goodbye to my family, friends, golf and rugby clubmates—and the truancy officer—off I went.

Thomson was as good as his word, and did indeed land a professional golf apprenticeship for me in the Victorian state capital of Melbourne, first at Rossdale Golf Club then at Woodlands. But I wanted to be a caddy, not a golfer, so I quit Australia after eight months and set off for Britain to join the European Tour.

Three months later and back in Australia, I attracted the attention of Greg Norman through my association with Thomson. Norman was looking for a full-time caddy, and I got the job in part by again being economical with the truth about my age. I told Norman I was 20, and the Great White Shark knew no better until two years later when he, his wife Laura and I were checking in for a flight at Hong Kong International Airport. Greg and I went off to deal with the luggage, leaving Laura at the check-in with the tickets and passports. Laura found out my real age from my passport, and told Greg. The subterfuge tickled Greg Norman's irreverent Australian sense of humor, and it's remained a standing joke between us ever since.

I worked exclusively for Norman outside America until I got my green card, which allowed me to work in the United States. I then stayed with him full-time through his most successful era, and became the first person to win a million dollars on the PGA circuit in a year.

When we finally split up after eight years together, I was approached by Raymond Floyd, and we were together for over a decade before the call came from Tiger.

Floyd had made his name at the age of 20 as the youngest ever winner of a PGA tournament, the 1963 St. Petersburg Invitational. He continued on to win the 1976 Masters with 271, which was a tournament record. That included 131 for the first 36 holes, a record that even survived Greg Norman's early heroics when the Great White Shark opened with a record first round of 63 and followed it up with a 69 in the 1996 Masters.

In between my stints for Norman and Floyd, I toted the bags for a who's who of international golfers: Michael King, Ian Baker-Finch, Wayne Grady, Rod Pampling, Craig Owen, Tom Sieckmann, Jerry Anderson, Sam Torrance, Sir Bob Charles, Michael Clayton, Terry Gale, Bob Shearer, Bernhard Langer, John Jacobs, Lu Hsi-chuen, Anders Forsbrand, Curtis Strange, Andy Bean, Jim Dent and Sandy Lyle, among others.

I also caddied for groups of celebrities, which included former president George Bush senior, comedian and eternally-thwarted golfing wannabe Bob Hope, and Oscar-winning actor and director Clint Eastwood.

I caddied on every continent and in nearly 100 countries. With my long-time pal, Peter "Irish" Fitzgerald, we even became the first Western caddies to work in China. I lived out of a suitcase for 10 months of every year before heading home to Auckland, New Zealand (where I'd bought my first house at age 17) for the Southern Hemisphere summer. I wore out a passport a year and racked up more frequent-flier points than a diplomatic courier. I saw the insides of thousands of motels and caddyshacks, and drove millions of kilometers from golf course to golf course.

Centenarian Caddy

In early October 2003, Tiger Woods won the World Golf Championship in Atlanta, Georgia, pocketing a little over $1 million, jumping to the top of the PGA money list, and clinching his fifth PGA Player of the Year title in the process. It was Tiger's seventh victory in 13 World Golf Championship events, and his fifth U.S. Tour victory in a year that, by his phenomenal standards, was not a particularly good one because he failed to capture a major title. But it was his 39th win on the U.S. Tour since turning professional, and it was a landmark for him because it equaled the achievements of two of the game's greats, Gene Sarazen in the 1920s and 1930s, and Tom Watson in the 1970s and 1980s.

But there was an even greater significance to the win in Tiger's eyes.

"People have no idea how big this win was," he said afterwards. "It's not just the Player of the Year or the money title: it was Stevie's hundredth win."

I had cracked the magical mark of 100 professional tournament wins in partnership with my hit list of the best players of the previous two decades.

And I was barely 40 years old.

The upshot of my century of tournament wins and two decades on the world's golf circuits is that I have come to understand, from a unique and practical perspective, the way the human brain—the mind—works in a high-pressure sports atmosphere. Because I had so little formal education, this understanding came by way of the sternest of teachers, real-life experience. I developed a unique model of how the mind has to be trained, not just to deal with the pressure, but to feed off it, to thrive off it. I know where Tiger Woods is coming from, and how he got there.

I have seen great golfers make themselves, and others, who might have been great, break themselves. I've seen the triumphs, the despair. And I've come to understand that the difference between the winners and losers is the way they train their minds for competition. I've seen that the sweetest swings and the biggest hits were of little practical value unless the player could produce them whenever and wherever he desired. That sort of consistency is a factor of the mind, not the body, the club or the ball. Some professional players train their minds for competition without knowing they're doing it, but most do it deliberately, to a precise formula and schedule.

Once I had discovered that fact, I realized that the mind itself is not the unfathomable mystery we're often led to believe. Sure, science has barely started to unravel the physical complexities of the human brain. It can't, for example, fully explain how pain and pleasure mechanisms work, nor even define where conscious thought ends and the subconscious takes over. But even so, my practical experience in the world of golf has convinced me that the human mind is a pretty simple machine to operate, and you don't need a college degree to do it. Once you know how to operate your mind, how to drive it just as you might a car, it can take you anywhere and let you do anything. I learned my basic mind-driving skills from Peter Thomson, and I polished them in association with the likes of Norman, Floyd and Woods, the best practitioners in the field.

And while all the great golfers I caddied for had unique temperaments, personalities, strengths and weaknesses, the heat of competition boiled their differences down to the same basic set of mind-operating principles.

Mental training aims to help the golfer reach a particular state of mind under the heat of competition, then maintain it throughout the day, the tournament, the career. Tiger Woods has his own special term for that state of mind. It's a feeling of unwavering serenity and infallibility. It's a sense of relaxed and unshakable certainty, during which the body follows the mind into a condition of heightened strength and precision. It's a state of mind that allows the player to freely and effortlessly tap the outer limits of their individual potential.

It's a sense of being 10 feet tall and bulletproof.

Tiger Woods describes this state as being "in the zone." Other terms for it might be "in a groove," "hitting your stride," "running hot" or "on one's game." The psychobabble term for it is "peak experience."

Call it what you like, but getting into that state of mind is the specific goal, the intended outcome, of mind-training. The peak experience, being in the zone, is what it's all about.

It's where success lies.

I have learned how to help get the player into the zone and keep him there, and perhaps this is the quality that gives me an edge over other caddies. I can't, of course, induce that state in a player just by picking up his golf bag, because being in the zone is the result of a structured training program that begins long before the player arrives at the tee. Occasionally, circumstances may arise that precipitate an untrained player into the zone, but that's just a matter of happy accident, and since the player has no control over the process of arriving there, he has no means of staying once his luck runs out. This is the difference that mind-training makes: it gives you the capacity to reach the zone by design rather than accident, and to stay in it despite the external factors which might otherwise tip you out of it.

Anyone can get into the zone by accident, but it's the masters of the game—those like Tiger Woods, Greg Norman, Raymond Floyd— who can enter it almost at will. And by dropping a judicious word or two, maintaining a constructive silence or cracking an odd joke to ease the tension between shots, I try to help keep them there.

That's what this book is all about: it's my formula for finding your way into the zone, becoming 10 feet tall and bulletproof, and playing to the limits of your potential, whenever you want to or need to.

Permanent Improvement

As I travel the world, I am continually asked by amateur players for tips on how to shave those extra few shots off their cards. I've got plenty of tips up my sleeve, and the best of them are in this book. But the answer I'd like to give to all those inquiries is that if there's a single difference between amateurs and professionals, it's in the professionals' mind-training. And I can't describe that in the few seconds it takes to hit a golf shot. By presenting my ideas on mind-training for golf in this book, I'm providing the answer I always want to give when people come to me seeking that magical insight into what would make them better players. There is no magic in my formula for training the mind for golf. No hocus-pocus, no snake oil. It's a dynamic world, not a magical one, and what happens in the future is determined by what we did in the past.

In this book I explain what you have to do if you want to get into a cycle of constant improvement. How far you ride that cycle is up to you. I am no preacher, and this book is no exercise in evangelism. It's a textbook of mind-training specialized for golf. You can pick up on my tips for immediate short-term gain, or you can get fully into my mind-training regime and let it carry you all the way to a professional golf career. The one thing that's certain is that professional golf is so competitive a field these days that no one can make it without some form of mind-training to complement the physical practice.

My target audience is the vast congregation of golfers of both sexes and all ages who simply want to play the best golf they're capable of. Whether you're a beginner wondering what sort of a starting handicap you can nail for yourself, an established golfer trying to get your handicap down to single figures, or a hotshot on scratch, my approach to the mind game of golf will work for you. My formula has evolved through 25 years working for the game's finest players.

For Peter Thomson. For Greg Norman. For Raymond Floyd.

And now for the one who may turn out to be the greatest there ever was, Tiger Woods.

2

Garbage In,
Garbage Out

If you can see it, you can hole it.

—Arnold Palmer

When I launched myself into the golfing world in the mid-1970s, the computer age had yet to dawn, at least as far as the general public was concerned. The personal computer didn't exist as such, and the tools and games it spawned were just glints in the eyes of the electronics engineers. How different things are today, with cell phones, PDA's and digital cameras all as common as sparrows, and the Internet opening up vast new horizons of communications and commerce. Where once I was limited to corresponding by airmail with my family in New Zealand, now I'm in instant contact by email and text-messages that are about as cheap as stamps. The breakthrough tool that produced these modern marvels was the personal computer, though it came into common usage only during the 1990s.

The working model on which engineers based the design of the personal computer was the human brain—a fact from which I extrapolate that the personal computer is a crude electronic brain.

Crude it is too, given that it'll be at least another decade before engineers can cram enough power and capacity into even industrial computers to make them perform feats equivalent to those of the human brain. The smartest chess computers today can beat a world champion player at his own game—at least sometimes. It'll be a while yet before they can always beat him, and longer still till computers are built that can beat humans in less structured mind games. So, as I see it, world-class chess players and the rest of us all possess within our skulls a super-powered personal inbuilt computer which, for its size, is the most sophisti-cated and complex organism/machine on the planet.

Given its immense power, the human brain is also the most under-utilized machine on the planet. Scientists trying to unravel the complex-ities of our personal, inbuilt supercomputers think that, at best, most of us use no more than a 10th of our capacity. Most of us simply don't know how to make better use of our brains.

Instead, we take a passive approach to them, accepting uncritically and unquestioningly whatever behaviors or performances they deliver. We tend to confuse the brain with the person, as if they're the same thing. In my view, a brain is just one of the person's tools, like an arm or a leg, and the person is the separate conscious entity that operates the tools. For my "person" you could read "ego," the term coined by the father of psy-choanalysis, Sigmund Freud (1856–1939), to describe the same relation-ship between the brain-as-a-tool and the brain's operator. I liken the chronic under-usage of our brains to people getting behind the wheel of their V8, but never exploring the car's full potential because they never venture out of first gear.

Yet it's this machine, this personal inbuilt supercomputer, that gives us the capacity to play golf. And by using more of this machine's poten-tial, more of its gears, we can play better golf.

This machine, this supercomputer, is so powerful that it's capable of analyzing, with a remarkable degree of accuracy and in only a frac-tion of a second, all the variables involved in a yard-long steel-shafted club striking a rubber-cored ball 1.68 inches in diameter and weighing 1.62 ounces in such a way that it rolls into a 4.25-inch hole in the ground as much as 300 yards away. In other words, this machine/brain that we all possess is at least theoretically capable of commanding the human body and its equipment to strike and sink a hole-in-one on any par-three hole and on the shorter par-four ones. Such a level of performance may be at the extreme limit of the brain's, let alone the body's capacity. But it is quite conceivable that the perfectly functioning human brain and body could return an 18-hole score in the mid-twenties, even given the need for extra strokes on the longer holes.

We're talking here, of course, about the outer limits of the human potential, demonstrating the size of the gap between what the brain is theoretically capable of and what is actually achieved out on the golf course. Given that par on most 18-hole courses is 72, we're looking at the brain having the potential to get a scratch golfer back in the club-house with only a third the number of strokes it presently takes. This gap between the actual and the theoretical represents the potential for individual improvement, and narrowing the gap is the aim of all golfers.

So, taking the perspective of the human brain being a computer-like tool, let's lay the parts out on the garage floor and see how they fit together.

Memories Are Made of This . . .

For humans and computers alike, the key to performance is memory. Another term for memory is stored information. The computer has two memory banks, one for short-term storage of information, the other for long-term.

So does the human brain.

During evolution from a cold-blooded reptile into a warm-blooded mammal, the human brain developed two new organs, which would ultimately distinguish our species from all other life forms. The first of these was the hippocampus, a mechanism for selecting and storing new and repeated experiences to create long-term memory.

The corresponding mechanism in the computer is its hard drive.

The other organ the brain developed during the transition from reptile to mammal was the amygdala, whose most important function was to allow humans to instantly recognize and respond to danger, by connecting current situations with the memories stored in the hippocampus. The amygdala, fed by the five human senses, serves a parallel role to the computer's Random Access Memory (RAM), which stores information that is immediate and transient.

Information passing through the RAM is processed for items that need to be stored long-term, which are then stashed away on the hard drive. In much the same way, the brain's amygdala gobbles up all the data from the five human senses and sorts through it for important items to be stored in the hippocampus long-term. The rest gets puts to immediate use before being progressively discarded.

Both systems start out in life—the computer in the appliance store, the baby in its womb—with a certain amount of permanent information already stored on the hard drive. In the baby we call it instinct, and it provides the capacity for basic functions such as breathing and suckling. In the computer we call it pre-programming and it allows the computer to respond to basic stimuli such as the keyboard.

Over time the amount of information on the computer's hard drive increases with the addition of new programs and selected data arriving by way of the RAM. So too with humans: the process of maturing adds new programs to those the child was born with, while its five senses— sight, hearing, touch, taste and smell—collect and feed in new information acquired from the environment.

The younger a person is, the more receptive his or her hard drive/ hippocampus is to new information, and the easier it is to store information there. As a person ages, the speed of hard-drive uptake declines in the face of the sheer mass of past and present experience and the process of maturation itself, which together clamor to fill up the most easily accessible space.

At birth the human brain weighs less than a pound, and will more than triple in size by the time it's seven years old. Thereafter it'll hardly grow at all in size, but the amount of data it contains will continue to expand prodigiously throughout life, whether or not we consciously set about increasing the uptake.

The brain of the modern *Homo sapiens* has remained much the same size since our evolutionary ancestor of a million and a half years ago, *Homo erectus*, started to get around on two limbs instead of four. But the amount and variety of information to which modern man is exposed has increased exponentially over that time, and continues to snowball.

So it is with memory.

Because the human brain grows larger only during the first seven years of life, this is the period when learning is easiest. The younger the child, the faster it learns. Essential learned behaviors, such as speech, become implanted in the infant brain's hard drive/hippocampus with a bare minimum of repetition, whereas in later life, new behaviors can be added to the permanent and long-term memory bank only by way of repeated inputs of the same data.

The Function of Practice

Loading the personal inbuilt supercomputer's hard drive with permanent and long-term data is the function of practice. In golf the single most important file of long-term data is that which contains the swing. We can talk about the basic swing being contained in a single and unchanging file of its own because the physical effort involved in operating it should not, if we're to get the best out of it, vary from shot to shot.

One of the first principles of successful golf that I learned from Peter Thomson was that each shot should take the same amount of physical effort. On a percentage basis, each shot should employ only about 75 percent of the golfer's maximum power. Variations in the length of shots will, for the most part, be accommodated by the different club sizes, and the physical effort should remain constant from one stroke to the next. I will have more to say on this topic in a later chapter on tips for rapid improvement.

Swing files are built up by repetition, which is what practice comprises. All golf strokes are variations on the theme of swinging the club through the same arc and plane. Strokes involving shortened backswings and limited follow-throughs can be contained in their own separate but permanent supplementary memory files, likewise built up by practice. So too for refinements such as fade and draw, but the single most important long-term memory file is the one containing the full backswing and follow-through. Sound coaching and regular practice imprint the basic swing on the long-term memory, and we develop supplementary swing files for the variations in exactly the same way.

For all that, no two golf shots are identical. Each demands a range of unique factors be taken into account: distance, trajectory and club choice, and external factors like the weather, the lie of the ball, the type of the fairways and the speed of the greens. In the computer, unique and immediate data such as this is supplied by the computer operator and stored temporarily in the RAM.

So too with the golfing brain.

The operator, the golfer, gathers this unique and immediate data by way of his five senses, and it's taken up by the short-term memory to be mixed with the long-term data stored in the swing files. This mixing of short-term and long-term memory data takes place in the mainframe of the computer and in the subconscious of the human brain. Output from the computer takes the form of processed data, while output from the golfing brain is the golf stroke.

To recap, we've so far identified three parallel parts of the computer and the brain. We've got two sets of memory files each: long-term (hippocampus/hard drive) and short-term (amygdala/RAM), and we've also got a mixing and output apparatus (subconscious/mainframe). Manipulating these three components to produce the useful golf shot is my "person," the computer operator.

Now let's turn to the loading of those memory files.

Loading the Memory Files

The process of collecting the unique and immediate environmental data for the brain's short-term memory RAM is called practicing awareness. When Tiger Woods steps up to the tee, he draws on his long-term memory files to provide the mechanics of his swing. Then he makes the conscious decision to add a specialized swing file or two, such as a draw or fade. Finally he draws on the data flowing in from all around him, including that provided by me, his caddy, to further modify the basic swing to suit the unique circumstances of the shot he is about to make. Then, combining in his subconscious the stored memory of his swing with the RAM of his awareness, he crafts another of the shots that made him famous.

The common failing of all computers—the inbuilt human ones as well as the man-made variety—is that they produce the desired results only if the computer operator has fed accurate data into them. Feed in faulty data and you get flawed results—"garbage in, garbage out," as they say in computer-speak. Similarly, our personal inbuilt computers, our brains, will produce the desired results (good golf shots) only if they have enough accurate data fed in, and—most importantly—only if we don't distort that data with extraneous thoughts on its way through.

Building up his own core long-term swing file by repetition, by practice, is what Earl Woods was doing in the garage of his home in Cypress, California, while the infant Tiger watched from his baby carriage. Earl practiced and practiced his swing. Each time he did it he added a little bit more data, a further refinement, to the swing file in his long-term hard-drive memory bank. Come the day when he went out on the course, he had only to add the unique and immediate data—the lie, the distance, the weather and all the rest of it—to the hard-drive data he'd built up in his garage. With that he became a successful golfer within the parameters of his own potential.

And, inadvertently or otherwise, he implanted in Tiger's mind the germ of the potential to become the greatest the world had seen.

I will have more to offer later on the techniques involved in combining the permanent hard-drive data and the transient RAM data to create the shot. For now though, let's switch our attention to acquiring the unique, immediate and short-term RAM data by way of our five senses.

Practicing Awareness

To reduce the number of shots it takes us to get that little white ball into that little round hole, we first have to develop the habit of supplying our brains with clear and accurate information from the immediate environment. That is, we must practice awareness.

This is an exercise in opening up our senses so they work like a sponge, absorbing every little piece of information that our environment can yield. We soak up details of the lie of the ball—how deep it's sitting in the sward, how much moisture there is around it, how long or short the grass is—and of the direction we intend to hit it in. We soak up details of the wind strength and angle, of the hazards, traps and obstacles to be avoided, of the point where we want the ball to land, and how far we want it to roll.

We soak up all this detail like a sponge, like blotting paper, and we do it without ever engaging our conscious mind. We simply open our senses to any factor, no matter how minor, that might affect the forthcoming stroke, and in doing so we deliberately refrain from making any value judgment on the data we collect. We never, for example, allow ourselves to interpret the ball's lie as either bad or good, hard or easy. Such judgments are irrelevant at best and destructive at worst. The lie's the lie. You've got to play the ball the way it lies and, because the rules generally don't let you change it, it's a waste of precious time and effort to let your conscious mind interfere with your RAM by trying to decide whether it's a good lie or a bad one.

As we progress through my analysis of the mind game of golf, this ability to switch off your conscious self, and rely on your RAM to feed your subconscious, your mainframe, with clear and unadulterated data will be seen as increasingly important—indeed, pivotal.

This switching mechanism is developed by practice—it doesn't come naturally—and it's essential to the operation of the personal inbuilt supercomputer.

The Next Shot Is the Only One That Counts

One of the strengths of all great golfers is that they approach each shot in isolation. Everything that has gone before is irrelevant—there's nothing you can do about the past. Likewise, the greatest influence you can have on the future rests on the shot you're about to make. Accordingly, top golfers exclude everything from their consciousness except the upcoming shot. They specifically exclude the shot's significance to their overall standing in the game or tournament. They view each shot as a separate challenge unconnected to anything that may have happened before, or to anything that may follow.

In the top golfers' eyes all shots are equal, and none is more equal than the others—something that fits nicely into my native Kiwi egalitarianism. And since all golf shots are equal, there's no point in making value judgments on them. The top golfers just gather the data, and deliberately suppress any tendency to be either encouraged or discouraged by it. It's just data: it doesn't have a moral value.

Sigmund Freud used to postulate the existence of a separate conscience guiding the ego (equivalent to my idea of the "person"). Freud called this conscience the "superego." In my model of the golfing mind we arbitrarily lump the superego in with the ego as a single consciousness, a single computer operator. Students of Freud may recognize our deliberate suspension of value judgments on observed data as conscious suppression of the superego. Call it what you like. In the end it's all the same, whether or not Freud was right about the ego and superego being separate entities.

When I was caddying for Greg Norman, the Great White Shark used to operate this suspension-of-value-judgment principle almost to a fault. He was so good at excluding extraneous judgments irrelevant to the shot in hand that he frequently had to ask me what his score was as the round progressed. This was so he could add considerations of match strategy to the sensory awareness he was practicing, not because the information was otherwise of any intrinsic relevance to his next shot.

The On/Off Consciousness Switch

The reason it's so important to develop a mechanism for switching off the conscious mind is because the brain will make use of every bit of data it's fed, whether it's useful or not. The only data it actually needs is the accurate, factual information required to perform the task at hand, and supplied through the senses directly to the subconscious. If the conscious mind is permitted to add value judgments to the flow of data, the judgments themselves become a distorting part of the data.

The subconscious can't weed out the useful from the useless. When it comes to composing the golf stroke, it employs all the data available to it, good and bad. So if the RAM data comes in full of distorting conscious value judgments, they become part of the resultant shot—and the garbage data coming in will make for a garbage golf stroke going out.

Confusing data results in confused shot-making.

Practicing awareness—that is, gathering the RAM data—is a passive exercise. It's a case of just opening the senses up to the environment, and letting all the data they absorb flow through into the subconscious without addition or comment from the conscious mind. The information going into the brain has to be cold and clinical, clear and unvarnished. It's the only kind of information that's of any value. Anything else just results in confusion.

Walking the Baby

To better understand how effective the subconscious can be in processing unadulterated information and using it to deal with specific situations, watch a baby learning to walk. Walking involves an extraordinarily complex series of muscle contractions and releases, programmed by electrical signals sent to and from the brain from all parts of the body. It's information that none of us was born with—we all have to learn it. The baby's personal inbuilt computer is undeveloped: it comes with very little data stored in it, but what it has got is not yet cluttered up with negatives and value judgments, such as self-doubt and fear of failure.

In learning to walk, the baby makes repeated mistakes, like over-balancing and falling on its backside, but each time it does so it's supplying its brain with new and increasingly refined information. The brain subconsciously mixes this information with that already stored in its hard drive/ hippocampus to make the necessary modifications to the baby's walk file until, finally, the baby can walk upright and go about wrecking the house and driving its parents up the wall just the way nature intended.

The important thing here is that the baby doesn't make value judgments about all the times it fell over while learning to walk. That's because it hasn't yet learned to make value judgments. The baby doesn't swear or throw up its arms in disgust or even get mad when it loses balance and falls over: it's too busy absorbing information—practicing awareness—to resort to silly histrionics and value judgments that do nothing but distort the information-absorbing process. The baby is simply aware of its mistakes and automatically trusts its subconscious brain to learn from those mistakes.

And the subconscious brain does just that.

To a baby, a mistake is neither good nor bad. It's just part of the information-gathering process and, as such, mistakes are as useful to it as successes.

Humans learn more in their first seven years than at any other stage in their lives because no one has yet taught them to interfere with their brain functions by offering opinion or judgment on the data being fed in. Babies are simply aware of what they want to achieve, and they allow their subconscious mind to learn the skills without interference.

The process of learning to walk is vastly more complex than the process of executing a golf swing. Yet a baby can so quickly absorb and process information on walking because its mental processes are not yet distorted by self-doubt and fear of failure. Sadly, it will pick up all these negatives later in life to a greater or lesser degree, and it will never again be able to learn so much so quickly. By the time the child gets to school, its learning capacity will already be approaching the decline that will probably continue throughout the rest of its life—unless it makes a conscious effort to arrest that decline by rediscovering the learning process that came to it so naturally as a baby.

By contrast, a lifetime of making value judgments puts huge obstacles in the way of an adult learning anything new. It should be a lot easier, for example, for an adult to learn to ride a horse than for a child to learn the same thing, but any riding instructor will tell you it's harder teaching an adult to ride than a child. You could explain this by saying adults aren't as supple as children, but the reality is that adults' natural instinct and flair for learning has become warped over the years by their becoming judgmental.

Note that it's the adults' *ability* to learn that's become warped, not their *capacity* for learning.

Remembering the pain of having fallen over at ground level, adults become alarmed at the prospect of falling from way up there on the back of a horse. So they bombard their subconscious with this judgmental information, this fear, and the subconscious responds by having them hang on for all they're worth: they tense their muscles, grit their teeth, clench the reins like a lifeline, and do everything they can to let the horse know they've no right to be on its back. The horse, being a creature sensitive to such signals, often responds by making the very thing happen that the adult feared in the first place.

So if you want to learn to ride without being repeatedly thrown off by skittery horses, you need to know how to prevent irrelevant value judgments—which simply amount to fear—from intruding upon the information-gathering that is at the heart of the learning process. The same goes for learning and improving at golf. Information-gathering is the essence of learning, and fear is the enemy of it.

In the next chapter we take a closer look at this fear, where it comes from, and the vital art of excluding it from the information-gathering process.

3

Packaging the Messages

The mind messes up more shots than the body.

—Tommy Bolt

In the first half of the last century, sportspeople relied almost exclusively on developing their physical skills and fitness to improve their performance. After World War II, however, it became increasingly apparent, especially to the Eastern Bloc countries of the Soviet Union and East Germany, that the purely physical capacity to improve performance had, to a large degree, run its course. Improvements in performance now came in 100ths of a second rather than minutes; in millimeters rather than centimeters; in grams rather than kilograms.

To get an edge over the West in the sporting sphere, the Eastern Bloc began to put just about as much emphasis on the mental aspects of sports competition as on the physical. As a result, Communist countries began to dominate world sports, especially the Olympic ones. Western countries, although initially slow to adapt, perhaps because of a lingering affection for amateurism, followed the Communists' lead, setting up programs to explore the previously ignored realms of attitude-related performance. The upshot of these was the emergence of the discipline of sports psychology as a key element in elite performance. These days most top golfers consult sports "shrinks" as the need arises, and some feel dependent upon them just to keep up with the competition.

Tiger Woods is an exception—the nearest things to shrinks on Team Tiger are Tiger's father Earl and myself—but I also readily acknowledge the value of the sports psychologist to elite golfers.

The great thing about sports psychologists is that they tell the player exactly how it is. Take the pro golfer coming off the course at the end of a bad day when he's made a few errors: he can try and sort the problems out himself or he can go to a sports psychologist. The psychologist will get in his face and tell him bluntly where the problems are in the player's head, then try to turn him around and send him off again with a good dose of positive attitude.

And attitude is the key to it all. Get your attitude right, and you get your game right.

This book is devoted to developing the "right" attitude to the game of golf, regardless of the individual golfer's ability or potential. You know you've got the right attitude when you've succeeded in entering the zone that Tiger Woods talks about—that is, when your game's on fire and you feel invincible.

And how do you know you're there? As we'll see later in the chapter on peak experience, you'll certainly know when you've arrived in the zone. It's like falling in love: when it happens, you're in no doubt about it.

The Key Elements

To briefly recap on what I've said so far, there are essentially four elements to every person's mental make-up. The first is the RAM part of your personal inbuilt supercomputer, your brain; this is the short-term data collection and memory-storage facility. The second is the hard drive, which contains all the data collected in the past by way of practice (repetition), and stored more or less permanently in the brain's memory files. The third is the subconscious, where the mixing of the two types of data takes place, and from where the instructions are issued to the body. The fourth is the conscious "person," which corresponds to the computer operator.

Complicating the relationships between these components is the fact that they all communicate with each other in both directions. They all both receive and generate messages. Most of this activity takes place outside our consciousness, and the upshot of it all is the block of messages containing the instructions sent by the subconscious to the various parts of the body. It's this block of messages that contains the golf stroke. If it contains only useful information, we get a useful stroke. If it contains useless information, we get a useless stroke.

We've seen that the RAM, which gathers the immediate and short-term data, has no emotion of its own. It responds simply and innocently to the messages it gets through the five senses. It will also respond, if allowed to, to messages from the person/operator. The same dynamics apply to the brain's hard drive: it can both receive and send messages which can, if allowed to, be interfered with by the person/operator.

The essential challenge of mind-training for golf is to prevent the conscious person from inserting useless interpretative information into the messages the RAM and the hard drive exchange with the subconscious. The conscious person is driven by a powerful desire to put a judgmental spin on the messages as they pass into the subconscious. Never mind that these messages from the person are of no relevance to the golf stroke the subconscious is trying to craft: they intrude anyway—unless we do something to stop them.

The RAM and the hard drive are just mechanical devices. Flaws in their performance can only be generated by the person.

Or, to be more specific, the flaws are generated by the person's imagination.

We've seen that the conscious person is the operator of the inbuilt supercomputer. We've seen that it's the source of conscious thought and choice. The imagination is a part of this conscious person. It's the part that makes humans different from animals and plants, because it allows us to exercise conscious influence over the kinds of messages we send to the brain. Plants and animals don't have that choice, or, at least, not anywhere to the same degree. No less importantly, the imaginative part of the conscious person also allows us to choose the sort of package—or the absence of one—that we send these messages in.

Just as the key to a computer's performance is the person operating it, so the key to the human brain's performance is the person, armed with an imagination, that's running it.

Evolution of the Imagination

Back in the days when we all lived in caves, the evolving human developed a capacity for self-preservation that we today refer to as the "fight-or-flight" syndrome. This was a choice of what to do when faced with danger: we could stay and meet it head on (fight), or we could run for our dear lives (flight).

But the important thing is this: we got to choose. We got to imagine. You can't have choice if you don't have an imagination. If you can't imagine the likely outcome of one action as compared to another, you can't choose between them.

Imagination and choice go hand in hand, and they can be exercised either with or without conscious thought.

With an imagination that could look into the future and predict the likely outcomes of the various responses available to them, humans were able in a split second to decide what course of action to take in an emergency. The appropriate response mechanisms would then be activated, and hormones such as adrenaline released to help deal with the situation.

Our choice of action in a moment of crisis can be either a conscious or an instinctive/reflexive one. Instinct and reflex are responses generated without input from the conscious mind, and they occur when things happen so quickly we don't get time to consciously sort out our response.

The need for this sort of emergency response doesn't arise on the golf course, though. Out on the course we've got plenty of time between shots to consciously exercise our imagination—in fact too much time. As we'll see, the challenge in golf is actually to exclude imaginative and conscious thought from the moment we address the ball.

But we're getting ahead of ourselves.

Environmental conditioning has seen the imagination evolve to such a degree that humans now recognize danger even when it doesn't exist. This is, if you like, the downside of having choice, of having imagination.

The worst manifestations of imagination unbridled can be seen in phobias like arachnophobia (fear of spiders), agoraphobia (fear of open spaces), and claustrophobia (fear of confined spaces). When the arachnophobic sees a harmless little spider, the imagination kicks in and identifies a danger even though there isn't one. The inbuilt supercomputer responds to both the immediate and stored messages without input from the conscious (rational) mind, adrenaline starts flowing, the heart rate increases, body temperature rises, muscles tense—and the phobic screams and flees. Sure, the fear is irrational, but that doesn't make it any less real. The phobic has responded to the irrational as if it were rational. Conscious thought, which would have identified the fear as groundless, was circumvented.

A positive manifestation of conscious thought being excluded in a crisis is when it drives someone to superhuman performance. The classic case is of the little old lady who suddenly finds the strength to lift a car to free a loved one trapped underneath. There are many documented examples of such unbelievable feats performed in crises by the most unlikely people.

What happens in such cases is that the messages collected from the senses by the RAM, and mixed with the memories stored on the hard drive, identify a desperate danger—in this case the imminent death of the loved one unless they can be rescued from under the car. In such an extreme situation the responses dictated by instinct are so clear, so graphic, so powerful and so urgent that there is no time for them to pick up the usual clutter of conscious doubts and negative thoughts along the way. They even fail to pick up on the common knowledge that little old ladies can't lift cars. Consequently, the little old lady performs a feat of strength usually reserved for only the biggest and strongest of young men. The effect of the RAM and hard-disk information being processed without recourse to the conscious mind is to trigger a response (in this example, brute strength) far more powerful than the person could have believed possible if they'd had time to think about it.

The capacity for such a feat was always there, despite the little old lady being unaware of it.

It's this latent strength, hidden within each and every one of us, that I aim to tap us into. This is where the miracle golf shots, the holes-in-one, emanate from. The aim is to train our minds to generate information of clarity and precision, while simultaneously excluding the value judgments generated by the imagination and passed on by conscious thought.

If we can firstly collect pure and uncluttered data from both our RAM and our hard drive, and secondly if we can exclude the imaginative spin our conscious mind tries to put on it, we'll be able to focus all the body's resources on delivering the most effective possible response to any given situation.

Just like the little old lady was galvanized into performing a phenomenal feat of strength under the pressure of an emergency, we all have the potential to blow away the self-imposed limits on our performance at golf. The elderly lady who lifts a car to free a loved one, and the elderly golfer who gets it all together to hit a hole-in-one, share one and the same experience. The trick to winning at golf, I believe, is to be able to tap into that capacity whenever you want to.

The True Nature of the Hard Drive

The role of the imagination in my computer-based model is central. It has a proactive capacity that goes far beyond the ability to recover memory files from hard-disk storage, or immediate data from the RAM. Indeed, the reason that computer engineers have so far had only limited success in duplicating the functions of the human brain is the difficulty they encounter in getting the hard drive beyond the recovery-of-data role and into an action-generating one. To make computers that are as powerful and versatile as the human brain, they'll have to develop a computer with imagination.

As we've seen from the examples of destructive phobias at one end of the scale, and of superhuman performances at the other, the imagination has both an upside and a downside. The first step in utilizing it to its fullest is to see it as a completely separate entity from both the RAM and the hard drive, which are essentially gatherers and processors of data. The imagination is a separate element in my computer-based model of the human mind, and it can operate either passively (in the subconscious) or actively (under instruction from the conscious person).

The imagination's active and passive capacities are separate not only in space, but also in time. The imagination exists in either the past (reminiscing about things that were, or might have been) or in the future (imagining things that might yet happen). By contrast, the short- and long-term memory banks (the RAM and the hard drive) exist and operate exclusively in the present.

Putting a Spin on It

Getting the relationship between the imagination and the RAM/hard drive working properly is the essence of my concept of mind-training for golf—or for any other facet of life. The relationship becomes dysfunctional when the imagination is allowed to put a spin—a bias, or a subjective or value-based interpretation—on the information it receives from the RAM and the hard-disk memory files, thus becoming a destructive factor in the relationship between the conscious person and the two passive information banks. This is because the machine-like subconscious acts on *all* the information it gets from both information banks, whether or not it's been distorted by the imagination. Instead of acting only on the relevant information—the unique and immediate data it receives through the RAM, combined with the hard drive's swing files and related stored memories—the uncontrolled imagination spins a recurring pattern of doubts and uncertainties that directly affect the outcome (the golf stroke).

The trick, then, is to eliminate conscious imaginative thought from the moment you address the ball in preparation for the next shot.

The Imagination as Enemy

To see how the uncontrolled imagination can produce negative results, in defiance of the body's capacity to deliver positive ones, let's look at one of the greatest events in world sport, the breaking of the four-minute mile. Early in the 20th century the so-called experts reckoned it was impossible to run a mile in under 240 seconds.

And for decades athletes believed them.

For years any number of famous runners hammered away at this magical mark, only to consistently finish a few seconds outside it. Then, just when the runners were about convinced that the experts were right, an English doctor named Roger Bannister stepped out one fine day in 1954 and, by more than half a second, proved that the impossible was possible after all.

And what do you know? That opened the floodgates. Within days no fewer than four other runners had duplicated the Englishman's feat.

Today a male athlete is nothing in international middle-distance running until he has at least a few four-minute miles under his belt. New Zealand's 1976 Olympic 1500 meter champion, John Walker, had actually clocked up 100 of them by the time he retired. Walker even built on Bannister's achievement by pulling off another "impossibility": the first mile run under 3 minutes 50 seconds (at Goteborg, Sweden, in 1975). Today the top male international middle-distance runners are knocking on the door of the 3 minute 40 second mile.

So how impossible is "impossible?"

Roger Bannister's achievement is probably the single most famous example in sport of mind triumphing over matter, and the lesson for us is that when the subconscious makes decisions on the basis of history alone, it's failing to recognize the body's limitless potential to rewrite it.

The role of the consciously organized imagination is to inform the subconscious of possibilities—such as running a mile in four minutes—

that it would not otherwise contemplate. Bannister actively and consciously employed his imagination this way, informing his subconscious of not just the possibility, but the likelihood of his body being able to run a four-minute mile. The four men who followed Bannister through the four-minute barrier had previously failed to so inform their subconscious. As a result, they could not run their four-minute miles until Bannister had run his.

When somebody comes along and rewrites history the way Bannister did, the subconscious is forced to accept that it *was* possible after all, and immediately the seemingly impossible becomes achievable. The reason Bannister's name, and not someone else's, was written large in history is that Bannister consciously used his imagination to inform his subconscious, in advance of his successful attempt, that the feat was indeed possible. The subconscious, that passive data-mixing and instruction-issuing machine, had no choice but to act on the positive spin supplied by Bannister's conscious imagination.

Ranger Rick's Self-Delusion

Like middle-distance running, there are clear parameters for success in golf. These include the handicap—or, for scratch players, the absence thereof—and performance in tournaments. These are the true measures of advancement in golf. There is also, from my perspective, a false measure.

There's a common term among the golf professionals about people who limit themselves to the driving range. We call them Ranger Ricks. You see them on the practice tees and driving ranges hitting balls from the same spot like machines, like robots. They stand in the same place all the time, and it becomes a repetitive situation where the conditions don't change, and the fear factor is absent because there's no penalty for hitting a bad shot. They may be stroking the ball beautifully under those conditions, but get them out on the first tee in a tournament and they go to pieces. There might be water to the left of the fairway and Out of Bounds to the right, and suddenly the mind can no longer deliver anything like the consistency the player was capable of on the range.

The Ranger Rick syndrome is another example of what happens when the imagination's mixing of the two sets of data—those from the hard drive's swing files and that coming in from the RAM—becomes confused by the imagination's capacity to introduce a negative spin. The output from the same swing and RAM data-files that produced consistency on the driving range is now distorted by the imaginary extra challenges that the golf course provides.

Facing a shot off the first tee out on the real golf course, Ranger Rick finds his imagination dragging up memories of how he messed up the last time he was in this situation (living in the past), or imagining the teasing he'll get from his opponents if he botches this one (living in the future). What's happening is that the clear and uncluttered data the information banks are supplying is being distorted by the uncontrolled imagination's self-doubt and fear of failure.

Let's see how this works in practice. Ranger Rick is up there on the first tee of a real-life golf course. This is the time when all that practice on the driving range should be delivering dividends. But as he prepares to make the shot, the information to-ing and fro-ing from his RAM and hard-disk information banks to his subconscious is being distorted by extraneous spin from his imagination. "Things are a lot different out here on the golf course than they were on the driving range," the imaginative spin begins. "Look, there's a bunker over to the left and it's out of bounds to the right. Worse, there are three other people standing alongside me, waiting to take their turn, and hoping I'll screw up the shot so they can beat me. What'll happen if I can't reproduce my lovely range shot here? I'll look stupid."

All of this uncontrolled spin is, of course, completely irrelevant to Ranger Rick's task at hand, which is simply to bring off a decent tee shot. His hard drive has located his main swing file, built up from all that practice on the driving range, and his RAM is delivering all the unique and immediate information available from the environment. He's got everything he needs to produce a good shot. The only problem is that his imagination is putting a negative spin on the information, offering useless distorting data such as how silly poor Rick's going to look if he screws up the shot.

If Ranger Rick could exclude the negative spin he's supplying from his imagination, he could comfortably duplicate off the tee his performance on the driving range.

Instead, deep in his subconscious where information is translated into action, self-doubt and fear of failure are being added to the information mix. And, because the subconscious brain can't distinguish between useful and useless information, it acts upon the totality of it, even those parts which are contradictory.

Informed that there is danger—the danger of Ranger Rick making a fool of himself on the tee—the subconscious responds by activating the fight-or-flight mechanism, the body tenses up and the adrenaline starts pumping. Of course there is no real danger—no more than the tiny spider offers the arachnophobic—but you can't tell that to Rick's unfettered imagination. The result is that Rick confirms his own worst fears by hooking his first shot into the bunker, or slicing it out of bounds. Had the useless spin, the product of the imagination, been consciously excluded from the subconscious information-mixing process, this wouldn't have happened, and Ranger Rick's performance on the course would have mirrored his ability on the driving range.

It's not the fault of the subconscious mind: all it did was to receive and try to act on *all* the messages the information banks and Rick's torrid imagination were sending it. What Rick should have been doing was excluding the fears, about both the past and the future, that his imagination was sending to his subconscious.

His subconscious would then have been free to operate strictly in the present, the immediate, the now, instead of being bombarded with messages of fear or self-doubt.

In short, Ranger Rick should have learned to concentrate on absorbing relevant information through his RAM—that is, practicing awareness—and allowing it to pass into his subconscious to be mixed with the swingfiles, without any imaginative spin attached to either.

Ranger Rick's mistake was a loss of concentration. And, as we'll see in the next chapter, concentration is an art.

4

The Art of
Concentration

You don't know what pressure is until you've played for five dollars a hole with only two in your pocket.

—Lee Trevino

Concentration is a precious state of mind—so precious that if you were rash enough to click your camera at Tiger Woods while he was in the middle of his backswing, your camera might end up entertaining the frogs at the bottom of the nearest water hazard, courtesy of me. That was certainly the fate of one camera that threatened to break Tiger's concentration as he was trying to extricate himself from an 18th-hole bunker in a nationally televised skins game in the U.S. in 2002.

I've never been wildly popular with golf fans—and certainly not to the degree that my predecessor with Tiger, Fluff Cowan, was—because I've always seen myself as a professional assistant to the golf star I'm working for, not a star myself.

And heaven help anyone who bothers my boss, whoever it happens to be.

A key part of my role as caddy to the highest-profile player in the game has been as crowd marshall-cum-bodyguard. It helps that I'm a big and fit man and have a background in rugby. All are necessary to play minder to global celebrities. Which is just as well, because Tiger is a magnet to fans wherever he goes, whenever he plays.

But it's not an aspect of my job that I relish. I'd much rather the fans kept their distance, or were at least considerate of my boss and the enormous stakes he's playing for. But fans are fans the world over, and I accept that protecting his boss' concentration from them is all part of looping for the Tiger.

There are those, among them many of his competitors, who would say the last thing Tiger Woods needs is someone policing his concentration. That's because, thanks to the conditioning that his father, Earl, subjected him to as a youngster, Tiger's concentration is diamond-hard. Earl's conditioning included subjecting Tiger to the same distractions that the unwise shutterbug employed when he fell afoul of me at the skins game—that is, making disruptive noises in the background at the height of his swing. Earl's purpose was quite clear: to make Tiger immune to such distractions. Anyone who has played against Tiger will attest to Earl's success.

Today Tiger is one of the least distractable players on the circuit, and the occasions when I feel the background disturbances are bad enough to threaten his concentration are few and far between. But the skins game came at the end of a long and arduous season, when both Tiger and I were as amenable to distraction as we are ever likely to be.

Concentration as the art of focusing so thoroughly on what you're doing that you can't be distracted from it, no matter what.

It's a learned art—not one you're born with.

There is a connection, of course, between concentration and temperament: some people are born with temperaments that naturally lend themselves to intense focus and concentration, just as some people have more natural sporting ability than others. By the same token, everyone's gifted to some extent, and today nobody gets to the top of any major sport on natural ability alone.

Of all the golfers on the European or American Tours, the one who springs to mind at the mention of ideal temperament is "The Big Easy," South African Ernie Els. The double U.S. Open (1994 and 1997) and British Open (2002) champion just happens to be one of those hefty, laid-back, easy-going people to whom nothing seems a bother.

The difference with Ernie is that he's a guy in whom tension doesn't seem to build up, so you don't see him letting it out with shows of frustration or annoyance. But the frustration and annoyance that are by-products of the game affect him no less than anyone else, and he deals with it the same way someone like Tiger does: he lets it out, and he gets over it. He just doesn't do it as obviously as the others because of the mild sort of temperament he was born with.

But whatever the player's temperament, concentration is an acquired, learned skill. Without it, performance will suffer. Without it, the golfer is at the mercy of the myriad of potential distractions—a gust of wind, an aircraft overhead, a leaf blowing across the fairway—that are part and parcel of the game of golf, and are lumped together in the rules under the term "rub of the green."

To recap on the description in the previous two chapters of the way the mind works—and specifically in the last chapter on the way his worked for Ranger Rick—we could define success in any sport as the natural and learned potential stored within the subconscious, minus the negative interference from the conscious.

The challenge to improved performance, then, is to reduce or eliminate as far as possible the negative influence of your conscious mind on the workings of your subconscious.

Left alone to absorb and mix the long-term stored information from its hard drive with the immediate environmental information gathered by its RAM, and then to transmit the resultant package of instructions to the various parts of the body, anyone's inbuilt supercomputer's mainframe (i.e. their subconscious) will always produce a golf shot that fully reflects their potential.

It will never fail.

Failure, in the form of a disappointing golf stroke, is the result of the conscious mind being allowed to intrude on the workings of the subconscious while it's mixing the data that forms the basis of the stroke.

The art of suppressing the natural tendency of your conscious mind, your "person," to interfere with the workings of your subconscious, is called "concentration."

Self-Confidence, Self-Belief

To realize our performance potential we've got to develop faith in our natural and acquired ability. In other words we've got to grow our self-confidence. We do this by feeding evermore pure and uncluttered data into the subconscious by way of the senses. At the same time we eliminate or divert the useless and opinionated material generated by that fearful little voice in our heads that is the product of an undisciplined imagination.

We all know that voice and the feeling that accompanies it: the tight, nauseous knot in the gut as we approach the first tee wondering if today's the day we'll finally start to get our game together, or whether we're going to fall apart again under the pressure of our own hopes and fears. These reactions are symptomatic of the old caveman fight-or-flight syndrome, which is still with us to this day, buried deep in our genes.

The syndrome is triggered when the conscious person perceives himself to be in a dangerous situation—the danger of making a fool of himself. "How will I be able to hold my head up if I mess up my drive?" he asks himself. "Will I be able to get my game back on track after that, or will I once again find that all the practice I've put in is a complete waste of time?"

The usual reaction to these feelings ("the butterflies," "nerves"— call them what you like) is to vow and declare to *try harder*, to *concentrate harder*.

And that's the great mistake.

The fact is that trying harder to avoid failure is a surefire way of bringing it about. If you have to *try* to concentrate, you're not concentrating.

Instead of responding to our nerves by *trying* to concentrate on playing well, we need to step back a little and give some thought to what's actually going on inside us. Our conscious self has become convinced that there's a danger ahead—even though that's plain nonsense. What danger? Is the world going to fall apart if we botch our drive, knock it out of bounds, find the bunker or the water hazard? Is making a hash of a golf shot going to trigger a war in a distant continent? We need to say to ourselves, "Come on, get real. Get a life." Whether it be a pre-season practice round with friends or the final day of a major tournament, the world's going to go on its merry way regardless of how we play. The sun will rise again tomorrow. Life will go on.

Thinking this way is the first step towards taking control of those powerful feelings emanating from the fringes of our consciousness. It puts the feelings in perspective, in their true place within our world and the wider world. It gives us the breathing space to realize all that's happening is that our hyperactive instinct for self-preservation has perceived a danger that doesn't exist, and it's turning loose all those old caveman fight-or-flight chemicals inside us.

In giving free rein to illogical fears, the conscious "person," the ego, is unwittingly defeating the purpose of our taking up the game in the first place, which is to enjoy ourselves. What's the point in playing a game—any game—that not only renders us sick with the fear of losing, but pretty well guarantees we'll lose because that fear has taken control of us? What's the point in stepping out for a game, especially an important one, if all we wished was that it was over before it started, or that we knew the outcome in advance so we could start coming to terms with the inevitable disappointment right away?

Where's the enjoyment in that?

We're supposed to be playing this game for the fun of it, for the appreciation of the competition, the challenge, and the joy of constant improvement.

Choking

At this point we have to step aside from our discussion of the art of concentration to deal with a situation that has caused me much grief and annoyance over the years. If there's one certain way of getting under my skin—other than by clicking a camera in the middle of Tiger Woods' backswing—it's by mentioning the term "choker" in the same breath as the name Greg Norman.

Personally, I hate the word. I get quite abusive of people who come up to me, knowing my past association with Greg, and use that word in reference to him. It's just plain unfair. How could anyone who's won 80-odd tournaments worldwide, including two British Opens and 18 on the PGA circuit, be saddled with a loser's label like that? They don't call Arnold Palmer a choker for finishing second in the U.S. Open four times and in the Masters twice, and for never doing any better than second in the PGA.

The basis for the label that I find so objectionable was the Great White Shark's loss to Nick Faldo in the final round of the 1996 Masters. After opening the tournament with a record round of 63, and leading by six going into the final round, Norman collapsed for a 78 to Faldo's 67 in that round. Greg and I had stopped working together by then, but the 1996 stutter was hailed by Norman's detractors as a reprise of 10 years earlier when he led into the final round of all four majors, but won only the British Open.

As everyone knows, the history of golf is littered with people who made it to the brink of the big time, only to falter at the final hurdle. But that wasn't the case with Norman: he had already made the big time and he completely dominated the game in the late 1980s and early 1990s. He broke the $1 million winnings mark in four of the years between 1990 and 1995, and even as late as 1999 he was showing the rest of the world the way by becoming the first player to exceed $12 million in PGA career earnings.

"Choking" is a vicious term, and to try to stick that label on someone as great as Greg for an admittedly unfortunate finish in a single major that late in his career is just so unfair. It really makes me mad to hear people refer to him in that way. Nobody called Greg a choker back in 1986 when we won the British Open at Turnberry but missed out on the other three majors, mainly thanks to other people's inspired play. No one called him a choker in 1988 when he went into the final round of the Masters 11 shots off the pace, then birdied six holes on the front nine and three on the back to finish just four adrift of the winner, Sandy Lyle.

Norman won plaudits all around for his graciousness in his loss to Nick Faldo in the 1996 Masters, offering no explanation for his unaccountable slump in form in the last round. He certainly had a convincing explanation available, had he been so small-minded as to try to diminish the greatness of Faldo's victory. For the fact is that, from the mid-1990s on, Norman was increasingly troubled by injury, but kept on playing in spite of it.

Eventually his problems became so bad that in 1998 he briefly quit the Tour to have bone spurs, which were causing tendonitis in his left shoulder, shaved off in an operation. Two years later he was hospitalized again, this time for arthroscopic surgery for hip pains that had troubled him for years.

In the first couple of years I was with Greg we won eight of the 13 Australasian PGA tournaments he entered. How can you call such a consistent winner a choker? It beats me.

The defense of my old friend and former employer aside, I acknowledge that the phenomenon of "choking"—regularly and consistently squandering in the final holes an advantage built up over the early ones—does exist. The worst-case scenarios are when people are so completely victimized by intense feelings of self-doubt and fear of failure that they are in the grip of a phobia. They suffer the same overwhelming reaction as the arachnophobic confronted by a spider, the agoraphobic marooned in a vast landscape, or the claustrophobic stuck in a tiny cupboard.

In all but the worst cases the choker syndrome can be overcome, firstly by understanding the mechanics of it, then by attacking it with a specific mind-training program aimed at turning the liability into a high-performing asset. The sportsperson with a bad case of the butterflies is simply undergoing a natural, though exaggerated, reaction to the pressure of competition, but it's a condition with potentially enormous benefits to their concentration and performance. All they have to do is harness that potential.

Changing the choking reaction from a liability to an asset is simply a matter of mind-training technique. The first step is to put those irrational fears into a rational perspective, as we did earlier.

The second step is to make those irrational fears work for you, instead of against you.

So what *should* be going through your mind as you approach a match?

Your only concern should be to allow your senses (your RAM) to collect and feed pure and uncluttered data into your subconscious. You do this by suspending conscious thought—the tendency of the imaginative person to trigger the fight-or-flight reaction, to indulge in negative futurising, or to wallow in an unhappy past.

Your real need is to play in the present.

In the Now

Golf's a stop-start affair—the second or so it takes to execute a shot is followed by long minutes during which you wait for other players to take their turn, and then you're walking or riding up to the next shot. The game is thus a succession of intense and brief periods of activity followed by long breaks. This pattern dictates your strategy for operating your brain, your personal inbuilt supercomputer.

And what you do is as follows.

The shot-making cycle begins perhaps a minute—no longer—before you step up to address the ball. You deliberately switch off your conscious thought by giving complete sway to your five senses—or as many of them as you can gainfully employ—to absorb every tiny nuance about the physical environment in which the shot is to be played. You listen to, feel—even taste and smell—the physical atmosphere about you, from the stirrings of the breeze, if any, to the temperature and dryness or dampness of the air, to the sounds reaching you from both close by and far away.

And, most importantly, you look.

You look first at the lie of the ball, taking in every last detail, from the way it sits, to the potential obstacles immediately around it, including any foreign matter it might have picked up.

Next you check the freedom or otherwise of your swing: is there anything behind, in front or above—branches, leaves, divots—that could interfere with the trajectory of the clubhead through the ball. Now you take up your position back from the ball, settle comfortably into it, and take a practice swing or two to let your subconscious know it's time to retrieve the swing files from the long-term memory bank.

At this point, with all your RAM senses still on maximum passive alert, lock your vision onto where you want the ball firstly to land, and finally to end up. Stare into that perspective for a good 10 seconds, allowing your RAM to passively mop up every relevant detail of the environment that it can.

Now address the ball, but before commencing the backswing take one last look at where you want it to go and, as best you can with your eyes still open, visualize the ball landing there and rolling to where you want it to end up

I'll talk at length later about the vital technique of visualization — for example, I'll explain the need when playing an approach shot to always visualize the ball actually rolling into the cup, not just making it onto the green. But for now let's stick to the routine necessary for each shot, be it a drive, an approach or a putt, because routine is an essential aid to concentration.

So you've had your last look at where you want the ball to go, and you've visualized it going there. Now look down at the ball and lock your eyes onto a single spot as far to the back of it as you can see—that is, as close as possible to the club's eventual point of impact. This spot might be a detail of the manufacturer's brand, or a speck of grass or dirt. For tee shots it could be a mark you make on the ball for the purpose—remembering, of course, to tee the ball up in such a way that the mark will be (just) visible when you address the ball.

Finally, without ever taking your eyes off that spot near the point of impact, execute the shot.

That's it.

That's the routine for every shot and, once you've established it, it's vital to stick to it precisely.

There is, of course, also an overall routine covering the sequence from one shot to the next, and it goes like this: having made the shot, follow the ball with your eyes all the way through its trajectory and roll till it comes to rest, still keeping all conscious thought at bay. At this point you're still in data-collecting mode, and you want your RAM to be soaking up every tiny detail of the ball's performance until it comes to rest.

The Off Switch

Only then do you switch out of concentration mode and become a human being again instead of a computer-guided machine.

When you switch out, switch right out.

React now to the shot if you must, albeit keeping in mind that you're competing against other players, not just yourself, and revealing your game plan to them by your reaction to your shot may not be strategically wise (more on this in the chapter on gamesmanship).

This switching out is something that I, as a caddy, help my players with. As soon as the player has signaled an end to this particular phase of the game—that is, he's ceased following the ball with his eyes and ceased showing any reaction to the outcome —I start talking.

With Tiger, as with Greg Norman and Raymond Floyd earlier in my career, it's sports that I usually start gabbing about—any sport, that is, except golf. Greg was always happy to talk about rugby and motor-racing, Raymond about baseball (he's a Chicago Cubs fan) and Tiger about basketball (he's a good friend of Michael Jordan). They never talked about golf because the point of talking at all was to get their minds off the game at hand, to deliberately rupture the cocoon of concentration in which the last shot was executed. With the shot over, it was time to give the brain a rest by turning the conscious mind loose with conversation, even refreshments (another part of my job is to stock the golf bag with the player's favorite snacks and drinks)—anything to get the mind off the job at hand.

The mind should be kept off the job throughout the stroll or ride to the next shot. It's only as the player approaches the next shot that he starts to think, consciously, of tactics and club choice. By the time he's ready to resume his pre-shot routine, he's chosen a club and decided the way he wants to play it. Then it's time again to switch off the conscious mind, get the physical senses feeding pure and uncluttered data into the RAM, and place his trust in his subconscious.

That, in fact, is my definition of concentration: placing your trust in the ability of your informed subconscious to do the job.

By following this routine, the player gives himself the best possible chance of performing to his potential—and, incidentally, he gives the disconcerting appearance to his opponents of being relaxed and self-confident. Whatever the outcome, he enjoys himself because he loves the game and loves to compete.

I suggest deciding beforehand that if you lose the game it will be because your opponent played better than you did—and that's something anyone can live with. Once you can accept that you've really got nothing to lose and everything to gain, you welcome the pre-game butterflies-in-the-stomach feeling because you see it for what it is: the signal from your conscious to your subconscious that your desire to win is at the right level.

Through all this the importance of having a switching mechanism to successively disengage and re-engage conscious thought will have become apparent. You develop this mechanism by a combination of visualization and repetition until it becomes a habit. This is what we'll look at in the next chapter, along with what I call the "snowball effect" that arises from the formation of habits, good and bad.

5

The Snowball Effect

My creative mind is my greatest weapon.

—Tiger Woods

Whenever sportspeople meet, one of the most popular topics of conversation is the patch of good or bad form they're currently going through. It's great when you're on song, with your RAM feeding pure and uncluttered information into the subconscious, and the subconscious responding with performances that are skilled, consistent and committed. But then along comes the form slump, which can be devastating for a player in any sport to come to terms with. It's particularly so in the case of golf, because you can't solve the problem just by upping the work rate: form slumps are a product of the mind, not the body, and won't necessarily be cured by a few extra hours on the driving range or practice green.

But form slumps *can* be stopped.

And then they can be reversed.

It's how you view the form slump, and then how you go about correcting it, that are critical. Since form slumps are entirely a factor of the creative, imaginative mind, the way to tackle them is with more and better mind-training.

First of all let's define the beast. So-called form slumps are the snowball effect of a decline in confidence.

To understand the process, let's go back to our example of the baby learning to walk: no matter how many times it falls over, its imagination isn't developed enough—and the falls don't hurt it badly enough—to slow the learning process.

Imagine how difficult it would be for the baby to learn to walk if its imagination was fully active, as it is for an adult. After the first fall the imagination would begin to predict more such painful and humiliating catastrophes and, in trying not to fall over, the ability of the subconscious to correct the pattern would be messed up. No doubt the baby would eventually learn to walk, through necessity, but the process would take a lot longer.

In other words, the baby has yet to discover the meaning of confidence, and the significance of lacking it. The kid assumes it'll eventually walk without falling over and, *because* it assumes that, it's naturally confident. It takes the falling over in its stride—literally. It seldom actually hurts itself—when you're only two feet tall the ground's not that far away, and your backside, padded with diapers, is even closer– and it hasn't learnt to feel humiliated when it loses its balance and plops back down on its bottom. Consequently, the information its RAM is feeding to its subconscious is uncluttered by fear of failure.

A human being's fastest rate of learning is immediately around birth, and it declines steadily from then on. A child is born with billions of brain cells, called neurons, of which only a relative few—such as those governing its breathing, its digestive functions, and the beating of its heart—come fully pre-connected. Babies often have to be taught even to suckle.

The process of hooking neurons up to each other (which is itself a definition of learning) is one of experience. Behavior is formed by cells, driven by experience, reaching out and forming pathways (synapses) to other cells. The pathways are strengthened each time the experience is repeated.

The pathways can also dissolve through lack of use. For example, Japanese babies, like all babies, are born with the ability to distinguish between "r" and "l" sounds when they hear them. But because there is no "l" sound in the language they hear their parents speak, Japanese babies quickly forget the distinction and, should they learn to speak English in later life, will tend to pronounce all "l" sounds as "r" ones.

By the time a child is two, the neurons in its brain have made at least 300 trillion (that's 300,000,000,000,000) connections, including the ones required for it to walk upright (though not yet to run), and to communicate in a limited fashion.

And it will never again learn so much so quickly as long as it lives.

The challenge for the sportsperson is to adapt the baby's learning processes to their own personal goals. This involves using the creative mind to build confidence by allowing the subconscious to receive ever-more pure and uncluttered data from the RAM. As the golfer begins to succeed, where once they floundered, their confidence grows and they become less likely to make the mistakes that delayed success in the first place.

This is the natural and positive progression of the learning cycle. But thanks to our creative imagination, which has an ever-increasing influence on our learning capacity as we grow older, there can also be the negative progression that brings about a loss of form.

Failure to overcome an obstacle can be either a positive or a negative influence in the learning cycle. Golfers performing below potential can either look at why they're making mistakes, with the aim of improving the aspects of the game that need work, or stew over the loss of form, and reflect on how things never seem to go right.

The path to success in any endeavor is always strewn with obstacles and failures, but it's how we react to them that determines the ultimate outcome. Form slumps are actually periods where the imagination has taken negative control over the RAM, and a negative snowball effect is in place. The more frequent the failures, the more active the imagination becomes; and the more active the imagination becomes, the more frequent the failures. The imagination, confronted by the pressure of competition with the timeless options of fight-or-flight, succumbs to the fears and runs away. The golfer ducks the competitive situation with all its perceived risks, and loses form.

The one thing the imagination can't overcome, however, is the conscious desire and determination to win that drives the player with the positive mental attitude. The road to mastery of any skill or sport is never-ending. You never reach a point in any endeavor where you suddenly break through the clouds to the blue sky above, and can abandon thereafter the mental and physical conditioning that got you there. Success is a never-ending pursuit. The dynamics of self-improvement are constant. Time and again we will fail but, if there was an end to the road, there'd be nothing left to achieve when we reached it. Desire would diminish together with the enjoyment of the challenge, and it'd be pointless to carry on.

No one completely masters their imagination, and as long as they don't there'll always be the carrot at the end of the stick to motivate them in their pursuit of excellence. They'll continue to fail from time to time, but will interpret failure as an opportunity to learn, to feed more pure and uncluttered data into their subconscious. As long as they maintain this attitude, they'll continue to improve.

To better understand the mechanics of form loss, let's look at what is probably the most famous case in modern golf. It's the case of a man that I caddied for in 1980–81, Ian Baker-Finch. A big Australian (6 ft. 4 in.) raised on a Queensland farm, he was still in his teens when he turned pro in 1979. He made his first waves by winning the 1983 New Zealand Open in Auckland, but people really began to sit up and take notice of him the following year when he led the field through the first three rounds of the British Open, only to slump to ninth with a final round of 79.

At a time when another Queenslander, Greg Norman, was beginning his rapid rise to prominence with my help, Baker-Finch bounced back from his British Open disappointment to take out the 1985 Scandinavian Open. He followed this up in 1987 with victory in the Australian Matchplay Championship, one of the highlights of the Australia/New Zealand Tour which, with the PGA, the European and the Asian, comprise the world's top four professional Tours.

The following year Baker-Finch displayed enormous mental toughness to force a play-off with fellow Australians Craig Parry and Roger Mackay in the Australian Masters. He took that title on the first play-off hole after belting a five iron to within a yard of the cup. The same year he went to Japan and won the ASO Open.

Clearly there was no pattern so far to hint at the problems to follow. He'd proven himself capable of coming back from disappointment, as in the 1984 British Open, and to be able to tough it out in play-offs, as in the Australian Masters.

In 1988 he qualified for the PGA Tour by finishing third in the World Series of Golf, and marked his arrival in the United States with a win in the Southwestern Bell Colonial. And he kept getting better. During 1990–91 he amassed no fewer than 15 top-10 finishes on the PGA and earned over $600,000, and it was in 1991 that his big moment came. In the 120th British Open at Royal Birkdale, he brought himself into title contention in the penultimate round with a stunning 64, so all eyes were on him in the final round.

He didn't disappoint.

In what is still regarded as one of the greatest finishing rounds ever played in that illustrious tournament, he birdied five of the first seven holes for a brilliant outward nine of 29 before coming home to victory with a 66, two strokes clear of fellow Australian Mike Harwood. His total of 130 for the last 36 holes was a British Open record.

It still is.

But just when Baker-Finch seemed to have the world at his feet, it all turned to custard. Suddenly and inexplicably his game fell apart. Some say it was because he tried too hard to get greater length in his shots in response to the challenges of the up-and-coming generation of big-hitting Americans and Europeans. Whatever the cause, the winner of the 1991 British Open plunged into a sequence of no fewer than 32 missed cuts on the tour.

The nadir, as painful as it was ironic, came in the British Open at St. Andrews in 2000. Teeing off with Arnold Palmer (Masters 1958, 1960, 1962, 1964; British Open 1961, 1962; U.S. Open 1960) in the latter's farewell appearance at the tournament, Baker-Finch snap-hooked his drive dead left across the neighboring fairway and out into the street. That nightmare beginning led to a nightmare round of 92, and the agony of it left him doubled up in mental misery on the floor of the Champions' Room afterwards. He was so devastated by the experience that he gave up playing professional golf then and there. He was quickly snapped up by ABC Sports and launched a new career as a golf commentator, so he was at least able to find another role in the game he loved. Thereafter he tried only once more to recover his form of old, when he fronted up for the MasterCard Colonial in the U.S. in 2001. He carded a 74 and a 77, missed the cut, and quit for keeps.

Baker-Finch has since added golf-course designing to his commentating role with ABC Sports, and in the interim has had time to reflect on his spectacular fall from form. His analysis of it is as accurate as his drive used to be.

"I was hooking the ball from fear," he said, "not from my swing. I was wearing myself out mentally on the course, physically on the range."

Of course there was no shortage of self-appointed experts only too willing to tell him where he went wrong, and to prescribe ways of getting him right again. It's impossible to say whether the decline could ever have been stopped: Baker-Finch's slump was so sudden and all-encompassing that it's hard to imagine anyone recovering. Certainly I'm not about to claim I could have saved my old boss from that grisliest of golfing fates, but what happened to Baker-Finch at least serves as the most dramatic example in modern golf of the downside of the snowball effect.

It may be that Ian Baker-Finch fell so far so fast because he had so much further to fall than most players who get caught by the snowball effect's downward cycle, and he remains the ultimate salutary lesson of the cost of failing to arrest the decline before it got out of control.

And in most cases it can be arrested.

The way it generally starts is with an isolated, but significant event. It might be one particularly bad round, or several moderately bad ones in a row. Either way it constitutes a serious enough slump in the player's normal game to allow a flash of self-doubt to enter the conscious mind, and then to penetrate all the way to the imagination. There, having opened a wound in the most sensitive part of the brain, it begins to fester. The imagination begins to intrude more and more pressingly on the role of the RAM which, working through the physical senses, is supposed to be feeding pure and uncluttered data about the immediate environment to the subconscious. Conscious thought—the "person"—begins to listen more and more closely to the negative interpretations the imagination is placing on events, and to project them onto the next shot and the next round and the next tournament . . . and so on. There can be moments which make the player think maybe he's at last broken the downward cycle and an upswing's on the way. But if that bubble gets punctured too, it makes the cumulative effect even worse.

That's the recurring cycle of the snowball effect: from good form to bad and back to good again, and then back to bad; from positive to negative to positive to negative. The possibility of recovery is stymied by the player's fear that his improved form won't last.

And sure enough, it doesn't.

Having allowed his imagination to inform his subconscious that he can't trust himself to maintain his good form, his subconscious responds accordingly, and the recovery of form proves to be only temporary.

The overwhelming majority of cases of loss of form can be reversed. The first step in making a permanent recovery is to accept that form—be it good or bad—is not an accident of the mind or upbringing. Rather, it's a function of the relationship between the conscious mind and the subconscious. If the imagination—the conscious and creative mind, the "person"—succeeds in putting successive negative and positive spins on the data the RAM is feeding through to the subconscious, the player ends up on an emotional roller coaster.

The problem can usually be traced back to that first incident, or succession of incidents, when the flash of self-doubt was allowed to penetrate through to the subconscious, and the player flinched in the face of it. This allowed his imagination to add an irrelevance to the package of data being sent to the subconscious by the RAM. The irrelevance was fear of failure. The subconscious cannot ignore any part of the information it receives from the RAM: it has no choice but to act on the totality of information it receives. And when the RAM informed it that there was some uncertainty as to the outcome of the shot, the round or the tournament, the subconscious was obliged to mix that information with the swing files it had pulled in from the hard-disk memory bank. The result? Good technique—as laid down on the hard drive by practice and repetition—plus bad data equals muffed shots.

Ian Baker-Finch's sad experience was a classic, albeit extreme case of his subconscious, his computer hardware, performing exactly as it was designed to, but delivering entirely the wrong outcome.

Of course the snowball effect has its positive side as well. It can also launch you on a cycle of constant improvement. The first step towards arresting the downward cycle is to come back to the core reason for your taking up golf in the first place. It's a case of stepping outside the square to look at your initial motivation, your initial desire. What attracted you to golf in the first place? Why golf and not some other field of endeavor?

This brings us to an examination of desire itself.

Peter Thomson, Greg Norman, Raymond Floyd and Tiger Woods weren't born with the desire to become great golfers, any more than I was born with the desire to be a successful caddy. Desire to do well at sport is the product of life experience. It may be a fleeting experience— a single tournament with a great golfer, as in my case—or extended exposure to the game, such as Tiger Woods with his father, Earl.

Either way, the experience triggers a response mechanism in the brain, bringing together otherwise unrelated strands of positive reaction. This flash of insight is taken up by the imagination, which mentally lifts the individual into the box seat of the experience, driving it, enjoying it.

Throughout life we experience billions of such desire reactions, most of which—like a sudden desire for an ice cream on a hot day—will quickly disappear into the past along with the experience that triggered them. Some, however, are singularly powerful and stay with us much longer. These latter reactions form the basis of sustainable desire and can lead us to significant, perhaps even great, achievements.

So desire arrives, and usually just as quickly departs, as an accident of the environment and/or the subconscious—something we experience—rather than as a fluke of genetics. Desire is a learned reaction, not an instinctive one.

And yet desire is the first and key prerequisite for success at any level, in any theater of competition.

This was among the first lessons I learned from Peter Thomson as a teenager, and I subsequently had that view firmly endorsed by Tiger Woods. My initial desire/ambition, like that of countless New Zealand youngsters, was to be a great rugby player, an All Black. But then Peter Thomson came into view, and suddenly one learned desire/ambition collided with another.

This is life.

It happens all the time, and not just in relation to big-picture desires and ambitions. It happens with little ones too. Suppose you have a desire to quit smoking, and are feeling extremely determined one day, only to have the desire vanish the next as the hunger for another cigarette takes its hold.

What's happened? Quite simply, one temporarily important desire has been shoved aside by a more pressing one. So what do you do? Sit down and have a smoke and a think about it? That's one response to changing desires, but if you go through life being led by the nose by a succession of conflicting desires and ambitions, you will realize none of them, and life will steadily become less liveable. To break out of that depressing cycle—itself a version of the snowball effect— you have to, at some point, prioritize. You have to choose what you really want in the long term over whatever's captured your desire in the short.

So how do you do that?

By first determining what's most important to you in the long term, then deliberately building up and sustaining the desire to achieve it to the exclusion of all else. This may seem obvious, but the important point is that you must make a conscious and positive selection of one desire/ambition at the expense of another.

Which of course raises the thorny old question of free will, and whether we've got one or not. It's one of the great philosophical questions of the day, and I have a perspective on it just like everyone else.

It's a position you could describe as dismissive. I am, after all, a pragmatist, and my position on this fundamental question is simple: whether or not we really have free choice in what we do, or whether everything that happens to us in life is the result of genetic and/or environmental conditioning, is irrelevant. You could spend your life searching for an answer to that question and never find it. You've just got to take the tools at hand and work with them, leaving the philosophical debates to the philosophers.

In the case of free will, we all labor under the perception that we are more or less in charge of what happens to us, that we are more or less free to choose any one course of action to the exclusion of the alternatives. Whether or not free will is an illusion is beside the point. We're all saddled with the illusion of it. We all have to make conscious decisions. We all make them. So instead of talking in endless circles about free will, let's just go on and exercise it.

That's my way.

My life is an expression of the freedom of my will. I chose to abandon one ambition in favor of another, golf over rugby. In doing so, I didn't want to be plagued for the rest of my life with doubts about it. I didn't want to grow old wondering if I could have been an All Black any more than I wanted to grow old as an All Black wondering if I should have been a caddy. It had to be one or the other, and the germ of desire that Peter Thomson planted in me was the one I chose to nurture.

That's the key point about desire and ambition: they may arise from accidents like the friendship between my father and Peter Thomson, but your response to them is entirely your own, made in the inescapable vacuum of human individuality.

And since you can make a choice between one desire/ambition and another, it stands to reason that you can make a conscious choice to deliberately nurture that desire to the exclusion of competing ones.

Desire may begin small, but it can be built into something big, something huge even.

And revising, building up and reinforcing the conscious desire that got you into the game in the first place is the first step in arresting the downside of the snowball effect.

Over the next few chapters we'll develop a series of practical exercises to reinforce desire. Using these tools we can ensure that the tendency of cyclical loss of form to become a self-fulfilling prophecy of doom for the golfer is arrested before it can take hold.

Of all the various mental techniques and systems adopted by top sportspeople to sustain their desire for success, and to optimize their performance, there's one you just can't do without. It's the technique of goal-setting, and we'll look at that next.

6

The Great Triumvirate: Desire, Concentration and Goal-Setting

I've always made a total effort, even when the odds seemed entirely against me. I never quit trying; I never felt I didn't have a chance to win.

—Arnold Palmer

It's as fundamental to success as wings to an airplane. You simply can't get anywhere without it, and anyone who's been a major success in anything will tell you so. It's confirmed by all credible research that's ever been done on achievers and the phenomenon of achievement.

It's called goal-setting.

Research shows that the top 10 percent of achievers, in any field of human endeavor, are goal-setters. You hear it from all top sportspeople—from Michael Jordan to Jonny Wilkinson, from Sachin Tendulkar to David Beckham, from Pete Sampras to Wayne Gretzky, from Tiger Woods and Jack Nicklaus to Annika Sorenstam and Ernie Els. They all say repeatedly that without goal-setting you can't motivate yourself to achieve anything. You may get flushes of enthusiasm that will keep you keen and focused for a few days, perhaps even a couple of weeks, but without conscious goal-setting you cannot exclude the multitude of distractions that inevitably crowds in upon you, diluting your determination.

The overwhelming majority of people coast through life without setting goals. But if you crave the satisfaction of expressing your full potential in any field of endeavor, goal-setting is a prerequisite.

Nor is there room for confusion between carefully considered goal-setting and plain old fantasizing. You can daydream all day about anything from taking down your loud-mouthed cousin at the local course to taking out a major, but that's not going to get you far down the track towards either. Wishful thinking is not goal-setting. How do you tell the difference? Simple: goal-setters write their goals down. Wishful thinkers never get that far.

What prompts goal-setters to write things down is initially a casual desire that they have consciously nurtured into a personal driving force.

Goal-setting and desire depend on each other.

The Desire-Concentration Link

As we've seen, my model of the mental side of playing better golf involves freeing the senses from the negative influences of the imagination, allowing evermore pure and uncluttered information about the demands of the next shot to be fed by the RAM into the subconscious. There it's mixed with the stored information in the hard-disk swing files to form the instructions to the body about how to execute the stroke. We've followed my game-management plan by deliberately switching off the imagination in the lead-up to the stroke, followed after the stroke by consciously switching it on again.

This necessarily makes the game of golf a mental stop-start affair.

The problem with this on-again off-again cycle of gathering information and processing it in the subconscious is that it takes a high level of concentration, albeit sustained over relatively brief periods of little more than a minute at a time. But those minutes of intense concentration mount up over the several hours it takes to play 18 holes of golf.

Ironically, the actual quantum of concentration required for 18 holes is less for a scratch player than it is for a high-handicapper, because of the difference in the number of shots each plays. Where the scratch player goes through 70-odd switching cycles, the high-handicapper needs 90 or more. By the same token, mastering my basic on/off switching technique will be of greater and more immediate benefit to the high-handicapper than to the scratch golfer. Or, to put it another way, the high-handicapper's rate of improvement will be a lot greater because there's further to go.

I make this point to emphasize that the greatest beneficiaries of his techniques will be high-handicap golfers: his techniques are not for pro golfers alone.

The problem with maintaining a high level of concentration, with or without the rests between shots, is how to sustain it. What's the key to sustained concentration?

There's really only one, and it's the desire to improve, to succeed. We can sustain a high level of concentration only with a high level of desire. To get our concentration up, we've got to get our desire up. And to get our desire up, closing the improvement cycle, we've got to set goals—written goals.

Golf has often been characterized as a game where one person's powers of concentration are pitted against all the others'. This is what the great golf commentators really mean when they talk about the outcome of a tense tournament play-off or matchplay final as depending on whichever player wants to win the most. Commentators like Ian Baker-Finch and Peter Alliss, big-name players in their own right, know what they're talking about: all other things being equal, the winner is always the person with the greatest desire to win, because they're always the ones who concentrate better. That's especially the case at the crunch end of tournaments or matches, because that's when the desire comes closest to being realized—or frustrated.

Now let's not confuse desire with desperation. Putting our discussion of desire in the previous chapter into the context of goal-setting, we can now define desire as the controlled and realistic focus on achieving a preset goal. Desperation has nothing to do with this focus, and rarely results in achievement. Desperation is mere fear, another manifestation of the fight-or-flight syndrome, a brief and passing surge of motivation. It's fear of failure.

Desperation is panic. Panic is a brief and fear-driven surge in desire.

Concentration, by contrast, is desire sustained without regard to fear of failure.

In a tight finish the player whose desire is strongest will stand out as being the most relaxed, as being the most focused on playing "in the now," as possessing the most powerful expectation of winning.

Tiger's Route

To succeed at any given challenge, your desire must have been cultivated to a higher level than that of your competition. True desire is not a passive or "received" quality. It's an active and acquired one. And even Tiger had to make the conscious decision on whether or not to turn the happy accidents of his formative years into a successful golf career.

Sure, desire starts out with an idea, one that lodges in the mind and grows there to a certain degree of its own accord. But, as we saw in the previous chapter, there comes a point when that spontaneous desire has to be coldly evaluated by the conscious mind and a decision has to be made on whether to elevate it to the status of a goal, or leave it to vegetate as a fantasy.

That choice is a conscious and active one, not a passive or subconscious one. It involves a deliberate decision, as distinct from a wishful thought.

Tiger Woods' development of his intense desire to win —an attribute that was among the first to impress me—is readily traceable through three distinct phases of his development as a child and young adult.

Decision One

The infant Tiger Woods, sitting in his baby carriage watching his father practice his golf swing in the garage, was exposed to the natural desire of most kids to emulate their parents. Kids are natural copycats because emulation is a key facet of learning.

But at that stage Tiger was too young to perceive any significant difference between his father's swinging a golf club or, say, a baseball bat. The geometry of the two swings is similar. But some time between watching his father and the development of his own physical ability to wield a club or a bat, Tiger opted—he made a conscious decision—to go for golf.

Earl Woods has said his underlying aim was not so much to make a sportsman of his son as to stimulate the boy's imagination to the degree that his subconscious mind would welcome physical and mental competition as an essential part of the life experience—which it inescapably is.

Whether the kid chose to do that through the individual sport of golf, or the team one of baseball, or through some other avenue of competition, was largely beside the point. Earl was out to equip his son with the mental and physical attributes to compete in whichever of life's later challenges he chose to accept. It so happened that Tiger, from the deep security of the trusting and loving environment that both his parents created around him, chose golf. The key thing is that Tiger, just like anyone else, eventually made a conscious decision of one course of action over another.

He seems to have taken the first big step down that path at the precocious age of four, about the time he made his first birdie (on the 91-yard par-three third at the Heartwell Golf Club in California). Earl obviously decided that, with this remarkable feat behind him, it was time the youngster took greater responsibility for his own decision-making. So he fabricated a test for him.

One day when they were about to head off together to the golf course, Earl hid Tiger's clubs under the front seat of the car, instead of loading them into the trunk as he always had before. When they got to the course and Tiger discovered the trunk empty, he demanded an explanation from his pop. Earl promptly responded that since it was Tiger's decision to play golf, it was Tiger's responsibility to pack his own clubs. Earl let Tiger savor this perspective—just long enough for the message to sink in—before retrieving the clubs from the front of the car.

After that, the kid, wanting to keep playing golf, made the decision to look after his own equipment. Whether he realized it or not, the toddler was making a conscious decision then to stick with golf despite the new responsibility imposed upon him.

Cruel and manipulative parenting? Well, hardly cruel, but certainly Earl was consciously manipulating his son to progressively take over more and more of his own decision-making. After all, the ultimate career decision—golf or something else—must eventually become Tiger's, not Earl's. And the lesson Tiger learned then eased the process of making that decision in later life. It's a common thread of the human experience that the later we learn things in life, the more harsh the learning process.

Decision Two

It was his 17th birthday and he seemed to have the world at his feet. A crowd of friends and supporters was there to sing "Happy Birthday" to him as he teed up for the final round of the Junior Orange Bowl

International Golf Championship in Miami. He seemed certain to beat a little-known Zimbabwean, Lewis Chitengwa, and thereby secure his eighth junior title on this penultimate day of the 1992 season.

But things didn't work out like that.

Halfway through the front nine Tiger ran into problems with his game, while Chitengwa excelled. Instead of refocusing and taking each shot one at a time, Tiger fell into a sulk. How could this unknown be putting pressure on the great Tiger Woods, the amateur golfing sensation of the decade? The further the round progressed, the more angry and petulant Tiger became. He eventually lost to Chitengwa, and salvaged only a little dignity by winning a play-off for third.

It was Earl's reaction to Tiger's behavior, as distinct from his performance, that really put the acid on the youngster. "The nerve of you quitting out there on the golf course," he stormed at Tiger. "Who do you think you are? Golf owes you nothing. You never quit. You never quit. Do you understand me?"

His father's reaction was a shock to Tiger, and it forced him to make a conscious decision about the game in which he had made his name. Could he continue in it without lapsing into adolescent self-pity when things started going wrong? Could he find within himself the strength to maintain his desire and determination to win even in the face of repeated and unexpected setbacks? Could he swallow his pride and learn from the experience?

The answer, as we now know, was a firm "Yes."

He had passed the second great challenge to the strength of his desire. He never quit in a game again, neither when he was struggling to make the cut, nor when he was so far out in front of the field that he seemed to have another victory sewn up.

Decision Three

The third and greatest of the tests of Tiger's conscious desire came in August of 1996, just after he'd won his third U.S. Amateur title in a row. He was ready to embark on his third year at Stanford University, heading for the college degree that both his parents wanted him to complete to secure his future. But the worldwide sports-marketing company IMG, which had been hot on his tail since he was 12, was now crying out for him to turn pro, and would eventually stump up $60 million in endorsement deals to reward him for doing so. So what was it to be? The higher lifetime security a college education could accord him, or the unpredictability of a career on the PGA Tour?

Like all decisions, in the end it was Tiger Woods' alone, and he opted for the golf.

By that stage no one knew better than Tiger Woods the difference between the fantasy of becoming a world-renowned golfer and the reality of it. His final step in becoming the greatest golfer since his hero, Jack Nicklaus, was in making that conscious decision to elevate his desire to be a great player above all the other desires clamoring for his attention, especially the one relating to his education. And so Tiger and I had a similar experience in making a decision between a golf career and education.

Cultivating Desire

The golfer whose desire is high doesn't lose his concentration, or stumble into the trying-harder mode when things aren't going his way. He trusts that as long as his RAM keeps gathering uncluttered real-time data to feed into his subconscious, he must be putting pressure on his opponents, because he must be performing at or near his potential. And should they loosen up at any stage, he's ready and eager to pounce on any opportunity they may offer.

Most golfers turn up at the course with no particular desire in mind except to do all right by their usual standards, and maybe pull off a win. If they don't play well it doesn't matter too much because there's always another game to be played down the track. Such players sometimes succeed, in part because they remain fairly relaxed about the outcome, but whenever they run into opponents with equal—or even lesser—ability, but with a greater desire to win, they're in trouble. They become aimless. They meander. Their play loses direction and purpose. They may experience success every now and then, but they don't appreciate, savor and enjoy it remotely as much as the goal-setting player who achieves something he deliberately set out to achieve.

It's a bit like the difference between the person who makes a million dollars by hard work and application, and the one who wins it in a lottery. The one who will most appreciate the million dollars, and will look after it and get the greatest enjoyment out of it, is the one who's worked for it. Which explains why so many lottery winners blow their windfall on one big splurge and end up financially poorer for the experience. The difference between the two is the level of desire they began with. The lottery winner had a freak win against near-impossible odds. The goal-setter was backing an eventual certainty.

To perform well at any given challenge, you have to cultivate your desire—much as a gardener cultivates a plant. The seed may have been planted by chance, but unless it's deliberately cultivated to the exclusion of competing plants around it, it will eventually be overtaken by the weeds of distraction that are its natural competition.

You have to feed your desire, weed it, water it and nurture it. You cannot sit back and just hope or expect it to develop with time. If you do, your desire will wither like an untended plant, eventually dying, then replaced by another plant equally short-lived.

Desire begins as a spontaneous notion, but it survives and flourishes only if it is cultivated. And sportspeople succeed at the highest level only if they cultivate their plant of desire to the exclusion of all others.

I work mostly with golfers who have already succeeded at the highest level and—in Tiger Woods' case in particular—want to continue doing so. But my mental approach to golf, as described in this book, doesn't exclude those who may not want to give up everything—family, career, other interests—for golf.

And they don't have to. That's the beauty of this system: it produces greater relative improvement in performance in high-handicap players than in the pros. The pro golfer can't do without this system, or something like it, just to keep up with the youngsters coming through. But the high-handicapper can confound his peers by producing a sudden, dramatic and apparently unaccountable improvement in form whenever he desires.

But whatever your ultimate goal—be it making the pro Tour, or just cleaning up at the weekly game by suddenly shooting 10 below your handicap—you have to actively and positively cultivate the desire to do so.

The Pen Is Mightier than Fleeting Desire

As a number of leading sportspeople will tell you, the first step in separating true desire from idle fantasy is to write your goal down. The reason is simple: your mind is filled to the brim with desires at any given moment—the desire to eat, the desire to rest, the desire for sex, the desire to have all your worries taken care of. These desires are with you all the time. So if you have a special desire, one you really want to realize, you've somehow got to set it apart from the myriad of everyday desires clamoring for your attention.

The way to set your special desire apart is to write it down.

This leads us to the best definition of success I know of—"the progressive achievement of personal, written goals." If you're not progressing in any field of endeavor as fast as you think you should, the first question you need to ask yourself is, "Have I written down my goals?" And if you haven't, you know immediately why you're not getting anywhere.

Setting goals and writing them down sends a clear message to the subconscious that you mean business. It gives substance to your important desires, setting them above and apart from the myriad of unimportant ones that are constantly buzzing through your head. The act of writing has a compelling effect on the subconscious because it employs so many physical and mental skills at the same time. The conscious mind has to select the right words from the myriad of verbal concepts stored as language skills on the mental hard drive, then forward them to the subconscious. The subconscious in turn has to convert them into the electronic messages that get the hands writing or typing, and the eyes overseeing. Writing is vigorous exercise for the subconscious, and the very effort of doing it impresses the message we're conveying deeply onto it.

When the opportunity arises to achieve a particular goal, and your desire is high, you can sustain your concentration not just for the first few holes but for the entire round, the entire tournament. With written goals you have physical evidence, and a concrete reference point, of your own desire to win. From there so much flows naturally: you are motivated to win and, to assure yourself of the best possible chance of winning, you become quietly confident and have a high expectation of winning.

The path to success for the golfer at any level becomes a progression of achieving one goal after another, each new one more demanding—and more satisfying—than the last. With written goals the player crystallizes his thinking, and begins to plan the desired progress as if on a map.

As the player moves along this path, the ultimate goal set at the beginning—and which seemed to be so distant at the time—comes closer and closer until the day arrives when the summit has been climbed.

Then there's the enormous personal satisfaction you gain from writing the word "achieved" over a written goal. Each time you do it you get a tingle—of delight, of pleasure, of pride (call it what you like but, like love, you only know it when you find it).

Whatever name you attach to it, it comes down to it being the comfort and security of knowing you've taken another step up the ladder towards your ultimate target.

Written goals are the first expression of your desire. With written goals *and* desire, you've got your foot on the first rung of the ladder to success.

The Goal-Setting Exercise

Now, let's get down to the business end of goal-setting. First we need to identify a starting point, because to achieve something later you've got to know where you are now. The best way to identify your starting point is to write down your answers to the checklist below. This exercise will teach you things about yourself you never knew you knew. Most importantly it will provide the base point for the charting of your improvement.

Nothing makes you think more clearly and seriously about your game than the act of writing down your personal history in it. If you're a mid-handicapper who takes nothing else from this book, this exercise alone will immediately shave a couple of shots off your score. The effect won't last for long unless supplemented by the rest of the exercises I recommend, but for a quick and temporary fix to an immediate problem with concentration, it's probably without parallel. It's immediately effective because of the signals it sends to the subconscious about the seriousness of your desire to improve, and the flow-on effects that will have on your concentration.

Further, this exercise makes it easy for you to identify both your strengths and your weaknesses, providing a clear basis on which to construct a strategy for improvement. Write as much as you can on each topic—at least one sentence per question, and preferably three or four—and keep it honest.

When did you take up golf (e.g. year, season, stage in your life)?

What made you take it up?

What did you set out to achieve during your first year in the sport?

What's your handicap, and is it the lowest it's been?

Have you performed better or worse than you expected since taking up the game?

How do you rate:

- your drive?
- your approach?
- your short game?
- your putting?

What are your particular technical strengths (e.g. driving, putting, bunker shots)?

What are your technical weaknesses?

What at your mental strengths (e.g. relaxed demeanor, ability to concentrate)?

What are your mental weaknesses (e.g. inability to detach from the past and play in the now)?

How do you relate to the people you're playing with/against (e.g. do they make you feel competitive, nervous)?

What's your temperament like? Do you:

- think positively?
- cope well with pressure?
- project an aura of confidence?
- react calmly to bad luck, bad shots, bad lies or bad weather?

What were the best round, the best hole and the best shot you ever played?

How do you approach a match against a weaker opponent?

How do you approach a match against a stronger opponent?

Do you go through form slumps, or periods of self-doubt?

How did you feel:

- before,
- during, and
- after that round, that hole and that shot?

What aspect of the game gives you the greatest satisfaction (e.g. winning, playing better than your handicap)?

What's your best shot?

How consistent are you at producing your best shot?

What shot are you not so good at?

What is your area of greatest potential improvement (e.g. your drive, your attitude)?

What game format (e.g. matchplay, stroke play, stableford) do you prefer, and why?

At what level would you like to be playing in:

- a month?
- six months?
- a year?
- two years?

Do you want to improve your game, and how important is improvement to you?

Just by answering these questions—and most especially by writing down the answers—you've already made a significant step forward: you've crystallized your thinking. You've brought yourself and your game into sharper focus.

The obvious answer to the first part of the last question is "Yes," but, predictable as this answer might seem, the act of writing it down is still a vital exercise. By answering "Yes" you affirmed your intention to improve, and in doing so gave formal notice to your subconscious that better golf is your immediate goal. And if your answer to the second part of the last question was "Very," you're reinforcing this positive message.

What you've written shows you what you've got to do (it identifies areas for improvement), and what you've already done (it proves you've got potential for improvement).

You're now ready to start setting your actual goals and priorities, but already, just by writing down your experiences in golf, you've significantly improved your chances of achieving those goals.

7

Goals—the Long
and Short of It

My goal is not to make a cut or just show up and play half decent. My goal is to win.

—Tiger Woods

Anyone who has embarked on a long-term project knows how the first flush of enthusiasm melts away as the hours merge into days and the days into weeks. Yet that initial excitement can be made permanent. It can be locked into the subconscious so that it's an ever-present part of your life. As I mentioned in the previous chapter, the trick lies in nurturing and cultivating your original enthusiasm and excitement, in much the way that a gardener nurtures and cultivates a tiny seed into a great tree.

This state of permanent excitement about a goal, which sportspeople refer to as being focused, begins with a master plan, a road map of small and moderate achievements culminating in a big overall one. Goals are the signposts of a master plan, and they need to be organized into three distinct tiers: short-term goals, intermediate goals and an ultimate goal. The resultant hierarchy of goals takes a triangular shape, with one single overriding goal at the top (the ultimate goal), a few in the middle (intermediate goals), and a lot at the bottom (short-term goals). Achieving the overriding or ultimate goal is thus reduced to a process of taking small and regular steps through the short-term and intermediate goals.

Because the ultimate goal covers the longest time frame, it's the first one to be identified and written down. In its highest application it can form the pinnacle of a personal lifetime master plan, but it is just as easily adaptable to shorter time frames. It can be as short as a few months, though more commonly it would cover at least a couple of years and, in the case of a teenager planning to become a professional golfer, it would need to cover a decade or more.

Depending on the time frame of the ultimate goal, a dozen or more intermediate goals may have to be set, each of them approached by dozens—perhaps even hundreds—of short-term goals.

Goal-setting structured this way delivers momentum, which can be defined as the generation of constant excitement in the process of achieving. With this structure it doesn't matter how far away the ultimate goal is—months, years, decades even. The achievement of every little short-term goal heightens the sense of excitement surrounding the ultimate goal, and reduces a vast and otherwise daunting achievement to a series of small and readily achievable ones.

The Golden Rules of Goal-Setting

Because the setting of goals is so crucial to the master plan, it's governed by a set of basic principles that I have condensed into seven golden rules.

RULE 1: GOALS MUST BE WRITTEN DOWN

Merely thinking about goals isn't enough. As we saw earlier, mere thought confines a goal to the realms of fantasy and make-believe, making it just another blip on the constantly changing radar-screen of daydreams and passing observations that occupy our consciousness from day to day. The physical act of writing goals down distinguishes them from fleeting desire, makes them achievable, and spurs you into action. Most importantly it alerts the subconscious to your decision to snatch something special from the never-ending stream of consciousness, and to elevate it to a status of pre-eminence.

RULE 2: GOALS MUST BE WRITTEN IN A POSITIVE WAY

No one serious about developing a success-oriented attitude can afford the poverty of a negative thought. If the goal is to improve your swing, it must be written down positively. Don't write, "I will not allow my head to move during my swing." That "not" is a negative, and there's no place for negatives in my scheme of things. Instead write, "My goal is to ensure my swing is enhanced by my head remaining still throughout."

RULE 3: GOALS MUST BE REALISTIC AND ATTAINABLE

It would be pointless to set a goal of winning a major inside a year of taking up the game, because even though it's theoretically physically achievable—from hack to ace in 12 months—the time frame is patently unrealistic. To even make the field for a major involves a progression through local, regional, national and international ranks that simply can't be accomplished in 12 months. There's not been a player in a major who hasn't taken at least five years to get there. This isn't to say that goals need to be cautious or conventional—far from it. But they've got to be realistically achievable in the end, and that includes being based on a realistic time frame.

RULE 4: GOALS MUST REPRESENT A TARGET NOT ALREADY ACHIEVED

There's no satisfaction in achieving again something you've achieved before unless, of course, circumstances have made a repeat performance vastly more difficult the second time round. The aim is to constantly improve yourself, your game, your life. Goals are the blueprint for raising your standards beyond anything you've achieved before.

For goals, look up, not down.

Raymond Floyd, for example, was looking up, not down, after he won the PGA Tour's Doral-Ryder Open in 1992. He'd already won the Doral-Ryder twice before, and 19 other PGA tournaments besides, but he was about to turn 50 and join the Seniors Tour. What challenge, what goal could the Seniors Tour offer someone who'd just won on the PGA Tour? But Floyd found a worthy goal: to become the first person to win on both Tours in the same year. We accomplished this in style, winning no fewer than three of our first seven Seniors tournaments.

RULE 5: GOALS MUST TAKE PERSONALITY CHANGES INTO ACCOUNT

You've got to be able to believe in your goals as your point of stability, of certainty, even as you ride the day-to-day roller coaster of your emotions. Accordingly, goals need to take account of the development of your personality—your self-confidence, your self-image—up to the moment that you set them.

Part of the process of moving towards set goals is being able to take increasingly large steps with snowballing confidence, but if right now you become a gibbering bundle of nerves the moment you pick up a golf bag, don't presume that's going to change just because you've decided to be a professional player. To make the pros, you're going to have to work your way through the factors—the onset of nerves when you pick up your golf bag, for example—that limit you at present. Don't kid yourself that there are no such limitations there in the first place. You have to recognize them before you can face them; you have to face them before you can change them.

RULE 6: YOU MUST HAVE A BURNING DESIRE TO ACHIEVE YOUR GOALS

Unless you're vitally interested in achieving your goals, there's little point in setting them. Goal-setting is about turning yourself from a thinker into a doer. Your goals should be something you're driven to, not just things that intrigue you for the moment.

How do you know when you're driven? It's a bit like being in love—hard to describe, but impossible not to recognize once you're in it. It's a combination of magic and certainty. In love the certainty arises from your natural genetic urge to be in love as a step towards reproducing, and the magic is the indefinable chemistry that starts boiling inside you when you're with the one you love. Potential ultimate goals can be put to the same test as potential love-for-life relationships. You ask yourself, "Knowing me as I do, and knowing my goal to the degree that I do, can I see us sticking together come what may?" If the answer's "Yes," you've got yourself a worthwhile ultimate goal.

RULE 7: YOU MUST BE DETERMINED TO ACHIEVE YOUR GOALS

Goals don't achieve themselves: you've got to get out there and achieve them. Setbacks, like form slumps and plain bad luck, must be expected and surmounted. Disappointments and failures have to be viewed as opportunities to progress, gaining ever-greater knowledge and experience, until each goal is realized. Achieving goals inescapably involves rejecting lesser options which may seem attractive at the time.

The techniques in this book are aimed at minimizing the sense of loss that making sacrifices entails, by heightening the permanent sense of excitement that closing in on a goal induces. But sacrifices still have to be made and, even with the best organization in the world, you're going to encounter those moments when you ask yourself, "Is it really worth it?" Having determination means the answer to that question will always be "Yes."

Formulating the Master Plan

Every goal-based plan has to have a yardstick of achievement. Golf offers two: the handicap and the tournament. For the part-time player, the handicap can be adopted as a simple and practical yardstick in the short term, but even at this level I am adamant that the ultimate test is the tournament.

Winning at golf is winning at tournament golf. It's not enough to crank your handicap down to zero by playing by yourself, or playing friendlies at the club, or blasting away on the driving range or practice green. The only way to truly measure yourself is to play in tournaments, because that's where the pressure is. Driving ranges and practice greens are useful for developing technique, but golf at any level is essentially about competitiveness—and pressure and competitiveness are one and the same thing.

Ranger Ricks don't win tournaments.

Given the tournament as the ultimate yardstick, winning a particular one is logically the subject of the ultimate goal. Handicaps and scores have their uses though, and they accordingly feature prominently among the lower-level goals we set for ourselves.

The Intermediate Goal

Intermediate goals are the major steps between a starting point and the realization of the ultimate goal. As an exercise we'll take the case of a kid in, say, his early teens who wants to become a professional golfer and go on to win a major. Obviously such a goal is simply out of the question for most golfers, who already have personal and professional commitments—not to mention the burden of more years than a teenager—that preclude such an exclusive and long-term program. But the master plan we develop here can be readily modified to meet every golfer's individual aspirations.

For our teenage wannabe major-winner, intermediate goals will represent his progress through club, regional, and national amateur tournaments, to professional, minor-Tour and qualifying tournaments, and so on to the ultimate: the European and American Tours.

The time frame for such a program would be in the order of 10–20 years. In this case the master plan would require at least annual intermediate goals and, especially in the early stages, more intermediate goals might be needed. It's best to err on the side of too many rather than too few intermediate goals, and there should be at least 10 of them, regardless of the overall time frame.

Our teenager's earliest intermediate goals should revolve around technique-based achievements, such as lowering handicaps and scores. After that they'll gradually switch to the real world of competitive golf by focusing on winning specific tournaments.

The intermediate goals should be written down on a chart, directly below the ultimate goal, and in descending order of merit.

For our ambitious teenager, the last intermediate goal before the ultimate one of winning a major would be to win a particular European or PGA tournament. This would be written down immediately below the ultimate goal. The lowest or first intermediate goal—say, that of winning the local club championship—would go at the bottom of the chart. He's thus created for himself a stepladder of goal-focused achievement up which he climbs till he reaches his ultimate goal.

The intermediate goals now have to be locked into individual time frames. Our ambitious teenager does this by writing beside each intermediate goal the date—it may just be a particular year—by which he expects to have achieved it. He leaves space alongside each goal in which he'll eventually write in the actual date and occasion on which it was achieved. He's thus able to chart his progress.

The chart he's created becomes his master plan. He pins it up in some place where he's going to see it repeatedly. It could be his bedroom wall or, if he wants to be private about it, the inside of his cupboard door or desk drawer. Wherever he puts it, it's got to be somewhere he'll see it several times a day, so that it serves as a constant reminder of the next goal up the list, and the progress made towards achieving it.

As a rule of thumb, if he were to find himself looking in a mirror more often than he looks at his master plan, he's got his priorities back to front.

This constant review of the master plan is a means of feeding himself positive messages both coming and going: he's reminded of the next intermediate goal coming up on his list, and he gets to savor again the satisfaction of having achieved the previous one.

The resultant master plan is reproduced on page 82.

Of course not everyone wants or is able to make the long-term commitment reflected in this particular plan. Most golfers simply want to express their full potential within the limits imposed by their age, lifestyle and other personal and professional commitments. But the principle of setting written ultimate and intermediate goals remains the same, whether the time frame is two years or 10, and whether the ultimate goal is to clean up the local club's stableford, or—as in the example we've taken of the keen teenager—to join the ranks of the perennial greats by winning a major.

Deadlines as Guidelines

So what if our ambitious youngster misses some of his deadlines? No problem. Missed deadlines are just part of the learning curve. They should simply increase his determination to carry on climbing the ladder, even if a particular deadline has to be rescheduled because he missed it the first time round.

Missed deadlines are not a sign of failure, and should in no way precipitate the abandonment of the ultimate goal and master plan. Rather they should be perceived as hiccups, reflecting the fact that there wasn't enough information available at the time of setting the deadline to be accurate about it. Missing a deadline simply means that the deadline wasn't realistic in the first place.

Exactly the same message applies to being ahead of a deadline as to being behind one, namely that the original deadline wasn't realistic. It would be patently silly to give up on an ultimate goal just because an intermediate goal was achieved earlier than expected. By the same token, it would be self-defeating to give up on the ultimate goal just because it took longer than expected to achieve an intermediate one.

Achievement is a factor of accurate knowledge. Being early or late for a deadline simply means the data used to estimate the deadline was inaccurate.

Early or late, deadlines contribute to the ever-expanding files of knowledge and experience contained in the mind-computer's hard drive. Early or late, deadlines are guidelines for making the master plan's time frame evermore accurate and realistic.

The following master plan demonstrates that the ultimate and intermediate goals can be expressed quite simply. They still have to conform to the seven golden rules of goal-setting but, as we'll see later, the real skill in drafting goals relates to short-term ones because they're both highly specific and personal, and not necessarily related to tournaments.

MASTER PLAN

ULTIMATE GOAL: I WIN THE MASTERS IN 2025.

INTERMEDIATE GOALS	DEADLINE
I win: A PGA tournament	2021
I qualify for PGA Tour	2020
I win a regional (e.g. Asian) open tournament	2018
I qualify for the regional Tour	2017
I win an open tournament	2016
I make the top 10 in an open tournament	2016
I turn professional	2015
I'm top amateur in an open tournament	2014
I win my nation's amateur title	2013
I win my district open tournament	2012
I win my club's open tournament	2012
I win my district's age-group tournament	2011
I win my club's age-group championship	2010
I get my handicap down to scratch	2010
I break par for 18 holes July	2009
I break 80 for 18 holes May	2008
I break 90 for 18 holes March	2007

The master plan, containing his intermediate goals leading up to his ultimate goal, is our ambitious teenager's blueprint for success. He looks at it, consults it, makes his conscious mind aware of it several times a day—hence the need to keep it in a place where he'll encounter it routinely and often.

He can update the master plan to suit unforeseen circumstances, and to account for underruns and overruns on the deadlines. Most of the time though, the chart will just hang where he can't help but see it repeatedly. It's best if he actually reads it at least once a day, even after he's come to know it by heart. But just seeing the chart sends another reminder to his subconscious of the priority it must accord to the goals on the master plan when it comes to finding space on the hard drive for new information.

Master plans are personal things, and each individual's is different from everyone else's. While the one above is designed for the teenager with all his top golf still ahead of him, the principles apply equally well to the veteran wanting to make a late-in-life mark at the social or club level, or the former hotshot making a comeback.

There's an important message in the flexibility of the system: success is measured by your performance as a factor of your potential. The person who has the potential to run a mile in four minutes, but who fails to do so, is less successful than the one who only has the potential to run a mile in eight minutes, but does it. There are no absolutes in the system, any more than in life: everything is relative to the circumstances in which it occurs.

Short-Term Goals

We now turn our attention to the fine print of the self improvement contract that we and our ambitious teenager are making with ourselves: the short-term goals. In their simplest form, short-term goals fill the gaps between intermediate goals, but at their most specific they comprise a detailed training schedule. In the case of our teenager, the more specific and detailed the better, because he's got so far to go and so much time to get there.

Because golf—even foursomes—is essentially an individual game, a thorough exercise in the principles of goal-setting, guided by the seven golden rules, will result in a training program geared to the specific individual.

Our player gets the process of establishing his short-term goals underway by asking himself, "Why haven't I already realized the first of my intermediate goals?"—in this case getting his 18-hole card down from triple to double figures—and then writing down as many answers to that question as he can think of.

He'll write his answers in a separate diary, not on the master plan, for two reasons—aside from the obvious one that there won't be space on the master plan for all the short-term goals he's going to write. Firstly, his written short-term goals will grow over time into an invaluable record of everything he has done to advance the cause of eventually winning that major. He'll be able to heed the lessons of his own personal history in the sport, and ensure he doesn't repeat the inevitable mistakes. Secondly, the diary will help his subconscious balance the filing priorities of the short-term goals against those of the intermediate and ultimate goals on the master plan.

Having asked himself why he hasn't already achieved his first intermediate goal, our teenager will have little trouble coming up with as few as three or four answers, or as many as a dozen, with which to start his diary.

Here are some of the more common answers:

- I don't have much confidence in my ability.
- I'm not consistent enough.
- I am easily distracted by the people I play with.
- As soon as I try to get a bit of extra distance in my drive I slice it.
- Too often I pick the wrong option, going for distance instead of accuracy.
- Three-foot putts unsettle me because they're so makeable yet so easy to miss.

In writing these answers down, our ambitious youngster has established why he has yet to achieve his first intermediate goal. What he's saying is that if he had more confidence in his ability, was more consistent, less open to distraction, better at making strategic choices and had confidence in his putter, he'd be carding high 80s instead of low 100s. In short, he's quantified his problem.

His next step is to go to each reason and assign to it a short-term goal aimed at remedying that particular problem. Given the problems outlined above, the following short-term goals suggest themselves:

- To grow his self-confidence.
- To become more consistent.
- To insulate himself from distractions.
- To swing consistently and let the club, not his own physical effort, determine distance and direction.

- To tie his hole-by-hole tactics into an overall game-management strategy.
- To insulate his putting from his conscious mind's value judgments about whether a putt is easy or hard.

In the context of the 16-year master plan our player has outlined for himself, six short-term goals is not many—especially when you see that he's got more than twice as many intermediate goals. But short-term goals are different from the ultimate and intermediate goals in that you revise them weekly. More on those weekly revisions later. For now, let's concentrate on this first list of short-term goals and see where they might lead us.

Write down the short-term goals again and, after each, write strategies for addressing them. At the end of the exercise, the following might be what our ambitious player would have written. Some of the strategies below are covered in subsequent chapters.

To grow my self-confidence:
- I'll adopt an affirmation aimed at attacking my self-doubt and fear of failure.
- I'll make a list of my achievements in golf so far, and relive each one in my head twice a day.

To improve the consistency of my performance:
- I'll develop creative visualization exercises.
- I'll check the local library and video store for titles by the top players, past and present.
- I'll routinely put in two hours' practice a day, either at the course or on the driving range.
- I'll play at least two nine-hole rounds a week.

To block the other players out:
- I'll concentrate on not allowing my conscious mind to influence the data being collected by my physical senses.
- I'll develop an anchoring mechanism that helps me exclude irrelevancies, such as sounds made by the people I'm playing with.
- I'll visualize my tee at the driving range as a cocoon that I carry in my head to the golf course, and into which I can retreat when I switch off my consciousness before I address the ball.

To control that slice:
- I'll remember to consistently put no more than 75 percent physical effort into my swing, no matter what the distance I'd like the ball to travel.
- I'll put in an hour a day on the driving range to standardize the effort I put into my swing.
- I'll set up a target I can reach and play to it with every club in the bag.

To refine my option-taking:
- I'll study videos of the top players to see how they handle particular tactical situations.
- I'll read discussions in biographies and coaching manuals on game management.
- I'll develop default options—automatic responses—to given situations.

To ensure I sink those makeable putts:
- I'll develop separate pre-shot routines for putts and fairway shots.
- I'll devote at least an hour a day to putting practice.
- I'll further develop my pre-shot routines to include mechanisms for switching off conscious thought, so my conscious mind doesn't make value judgments on each shot's difficulty.

What should begin to become apparent at this point is that the list of short-term goals is already close to being a daily schedule of activities towards your next (or first) intermediate goal.

Different sports require different training schedules. Runners, for example, have a daily schedule that prescribes the sorts of distances they must cover, and the effort (speed) at which to cover them. This sort of schedule can be a daunting thing, especially if it stretches out into the future. But if the schedule can be recast into a succession of short-term goals, revised weekly, they cease to appear rigid, long-term and burdensome. Short-term goals are flexible, immediate and satisfying.

We can now expand our ambitious teenager's list of short-term goals into a week-by-week activity list. Our youngster will set himself a particular time every week—say, half an hour every Sunday evening—

to sit down and write out his list of daily activities for the week ahead, based on his written short-term goals. Taking the typical six goals listed above, his week's activity list would begin to look something like this:

MONDAY: Meet coach for half-hour session concentrating on the swing and the drive; practice swing one hour alone; spend an hour on the putting green; watch a video of one of the greats; review master plan and affirmations just before going to sleep.

TUESDAY: Set up a target on the practice fairway and play to it with every club in the bag for an hour; spend an hour on the putting green practicing from at least 15 meters; play nine holes; do the mind exercises just before going to sleep.

WEDNESDAY: Meet coach for 30-minute session on putting; practice half an hour on three-foot putts; practice chipping for one hour; do the mind exercises just before going to sleep.

THURSDAY: Practice iron shots for one hour, five strokes each at a time, concentrating on putting exactly the same 75 percent effort into each; practice bunker shots for half an hour; practice putts of varying length for half an hour; read the first couple of chapters of a top player's memoirs; do the mind exercises just before going to sleep.

FRIDAY: Driving-range practice for one hour, concentrating on putting the same 75 percent physical effort into each swing; practice short irons and chips to a single target for half an hour; practice close-up (a meter or so) putts for half an hour; watch TV or a video of a recent top tournament, with a particular eye on the way the top players exercise their tactical options; plan game management for competition on weekend; do the mind exercises just before going to sleep.

SATURDAY: Play nine holes, concentrating on the mental switching mechanism to exclude conscious thought and value judgments from the information being gathered through the senses by the RAM; just before going to sleep, mentally go over the round again hole by hole, savoring the shots that gave most satisfaction.

SUNDAY: Play 18 holes, again concentrating on the mental switching mechanism to exclude extraneous sights, sounds and value judgments; apply to each hole the lessons learned from reviewing the previous day's round; just before going to sleep, mentally go over the round again hole by hole, savoring the shots that gave most satisfaction.

It's startling how quickly this sort of weekly schedule will begin to iron out the problems in our ambitious teenager's—or anyone else's—game. At the same time it gives a huge boost to the self-confidence.

Improvements will come fastest at the start of such a schedule, when the learning curve is at its steepest. The rate of improvement will inevitably slow after that, but our youngster will keep on improving, keep on achieving those intermediate goals, and draw himself inexorably closer to his ultimate goal, that major win. All he has to do is keep up the exercises.

The reverse will apply should he quit the regime: his rate of decline will be fastest immediately after he quits, and he'll get worse more slowly thereafter. That's the way the mind works: goal-setting and attainment comprise a progression of simple, daily steps towards a predetermined target, but the biggest strides are made at the start.

It's that daily sense of achievement that will get our youngster where he wants to go. Likewise for the 70-year-old with a two-year project of getting back into the game: the principles remain the same, and the goals are equally achievable.

Finally, a word about those nightly mind exercises (to be covered in later chapters). The time to do both these exercises is just before sleep. This timing allows the subconscious to continue chewing over the day's activities and goals throughout the hours of sleep when we can't do it consciously. To conclude:

Each night of the week we do two things:
- Check off each completed activity on the list, adding a few comments on how you went. For example, you might write against your entry for Monday: "Coach nails down slicing problem to my lifting my head at the start of my swing. Solution: keep the head still throughout." Friday's might read: "Yeah, I'm starting to understand which tactical options are the best to employ in which circumstances. The first test of my progress will be the game on Sunday."
- Read slowly through your master plan. We're already coming face to face with our master plan several times a day, because we've probably laminated it and have certainly posted it in a place where we can't help seeing it. The nightly read of our master plan con-

solidates the impact of seeing it during the day, and the subconscious will automatically reinforce the importance of it while we sleep.

Then every week (ideally Sunday evening), after we've prepared the next week's activity list, we need to:

- Review our short-term progress to date. Take special note, savoring and congratulating ourselves on any little improvements we've made. "That swing of mine is really beginning to smooth itself out, and is feeling sweet," or, "Hey, I finally beat that dogleg on the 13th because I hit the drive so sweetly it just ran on and on—fantastic!"
- Review our master plan one more time. This is a time to think back on the latest intermediate goal we achieved, remembering how it felt at the moment we achieved it, and what it felt like to check it off on the master plan It's a time also to think ahead to the achievement of the next intermediate goal, and how significant a step that will be towards the ultimate goal.

We've now got the structure of goal-setting and achievement in place. Over the next few chapters we'll look at the mental techniques and exercises that glue it all together.

8

Affirmations—
Schooling the
Subconscious

Golf is 90% inspiration and 10% perspiration.

—Johnny Miller

Tell someone repeatedly that the sky is red, and they'll eventually believe it. From Adolf Hitler and Joseph Stalin to Pol Pot and Saddam Hussein, recent and ancient history is full of ruthless people who controlled and exploited entire nations simply by bombarding them with lies. The cynic would point to this as proof of how fatally stupid people are. The realist would point instead to the old political truism that if you tell the people something often enough, they'll eventually begin to believe it.

The realist is right: the great mass of humanity is not stupid, but sections of it can be misled and manipulated by ruthless people.

This somewhat disturbing reality reflects the nature of the human subconscious. Like a computer, the subconscious doesn't have a conscience. Like a computer it accepts as fact, as reality, any and all information the combination of the conscious mind and the senses chooses to feed it, be it profound knowledge or arrant nonsense. The subconscious simply can't distinguish between the two, any more than a computer can.

This principle has sustained dictators, liars, cheats and con men throughout human history, and probably always will. There are dictatorships and oligarchies today that remain in power simply by controlling the messages getting through to their imprisoned peoples. As long as they can keep control over the information their people receive, they'll stay in power.

Sad as that may be, there's also an upside to the mind-computer's inability to distinguish fact from fiction, and it's one that demonstrates another vital element in the mind game of golf. It's a marvelous device for imposing ideas that the subconscious would not otherwise be exposed to—ideas like, "I am a great golfer," even though you haven't yet earned a handicap.

The device is called affirmation, and the mechanism behind it is repetition.

The area in which the human subconscious most closely resembles the computer is in its unquestioning acceptance of the truth of the information fed into it. The subconscious is incapable of making value judgments. Only the conscious mind can do that. The subconscious passively accepts everything it's told by the conscious mind, no matter how implausible.

If a message is sent to the subconscious which flagrantly contradicts something it's already got stored in its hard-disk information files, the subconscious will simply store the new information right alongside the old. The contradictions will sit side by side until the conscious mind either decides one or the other should be discarded or the subconscious tries (vainly) to fit both into the action-messages it sends to the body.

Let's take the case of the subconscious of a high-handicap hacker. Throughout the time he's been playing the game, his conscious mind has been informing his subconscious that he's not very good at it. The evidence appears incontrovertible: the guy's shooting in the high 100s. The subconscious accepts this information, and duly stores it away in a hard-disk information file. There it's reinforced by the evidence of repeated poor performances on the golf course. As a result, the hacker continues to hack.

But what happens if the hacker were to do nothing else about his game but to consciously start introducing information that is contradictory to that already filed by the subconscious? What if the hacker were to consciously send the message, "I am an excellent golfer" to his subconscious? Would such a blatant contradiction crash the computer-brain's circuitry?

No. The subconscious will simply incorporate this new information into the old, and use the lot to formulate its instructions to the body. One single contradictory message from the golfer won't put much of a dent into the subconscious' existing perception that the golfer's a hacker. But it will put a dent in it, and if the new message is repeated, the dent will grow.

In formulating its instructions to the body, the subconscious will incorporate both messages, and the effect will be a marginally less incompetent golf shot than usual.

Unless the new and contradictory information is reinforced by repetition, the subconscious will eventually purge it from the files—that is, forget about it—and go back to working on the basis of the old information. However, if the new information is repeated over and over, it's the old stuff that eventually gets purged, allowing the subconscious to formulate the strokes in the unshakable belief that the golfer is, just as he's claimed, an excellent one.

That of course won't be enough to turn the hacker into a champion, because every excellent golf shot is also made up of swing files created by that other form of repetition, practice. But what this deliberate misinformation fed into the subconscious will do is ensure the subconscious delivers a golf stroke that reflects the full potential of the information stored on its hard drive. The hacker won't become Tiger Woods overnight, but at least he'll be playing at or near his true potential. He might, for example, start making those three-foot putts instead of missing them. His score would begin to reflect the messages to his subconscious that he is, indeed, "excellent" at this game, at least within the limitations of his potential.

It's a deceptively simple process, but it works. With affirmations, we can trick our subconscious minds into delivering performances that reflect our full potential, whatever it might be at the time. Affirmations are positive statements of what we'd like to do or be in the future, but written down in a way that suggests we've already achieved or become them.

The Positive Versus the Negative

The human subconscious is wide open to suggestion. Using affirmations, the hack golfer can suggest to his subconscious that he's an ace rather than a rabbit.

The motivator Zig Zigler has another spin to put on this same phenomenon: if somebody came to your home and dumped a bag of trash on your living room floor, you'd be justifiably angry. You'd want the offender to clean up the mess, and you'd tell him he wasn't welcome in your home any more. Why is it then, Zig asked, that human beings seem prepared to let people dump the garbage of negative thoughts and ideas in their minds?

Fair question.

It's not just brutal dictators who use the power of suggestion to get other people to behave the way they want. There's the tall poppy syndrome—that tendency to criticize successful people, and a reluctance to experiment with new ideas—at work in most cultures. It's a negative conditioning that begins at school, where kids are subject to peer pressure—that is, to conform or risk being unpopular—and it continues right on through adult life.

Given that success is what you achieve in relation to your potential to achieve it, it seems that the people who are most ready to wield the tall poppy axe are those who never succeed in anything much themselves, but feel less uncomfortable about their own shortcomings if they're chopping down those people who do succeed.

We've all the heard the "experts" at the local club performing damning put-downs of prominent golfers because, at one time or another, they didn't like their approach to the game. Jack Nicklaus came in for flak because he was perceived as being too grim and serious when at work on the course; Lee Trevino because he never stopped talking; Gary Player because he came from South Africa at a time when it was locked into the tragedy of apartheid; Tiger Woods because he swapped a grandfatherly old caddy for a hard-bitten young one.

Of course nobody's above criticism, but people who trash the world's best golfers because of the intensity—or, in Trevino's case, the perceived frivolity—with which they play, or the ugliness of the political system in their home country, or their changed requirements for a caddy, are themselves almost always talkers rather than doers. Such tall poppy critics would have us believe that *they* deserve the winners' accolades precisely because of their own lack of success.

I can testify that such nit-picking from the grass roots does filter through to the great players. But one of the reasons they're great is that they don't let it affect them. To extend Zig Zigler's analogy, if the great players were prepared to let such self-important losers fill their minds with negative garbage, they might as well invite them to dump trash on their living room floors. Instead, what they do is filter out the negative and let only the positive get through to their subconscious.

This isn't to suggest that they can't take constructive criticism. Far from it. A major reason for the greats becoming great is that they're able to learn from their mistakes. But this doesn't extend to allowing streams of negativity to flow into their subconscious from self-serving wannabes. Rather, they not only learn to sift the useful criticism from the garbage, but they pass the criticism on to their subconscious in a positive form, not a negative one. They don't say, "There's a wobble in my swing." They say, "My swing is smooth as silk." If they were admit to their subconscious that there was a problem with their swing, it'd be tantamount to locking the problem in place. Instead they bring the need for a smoother swing to their subconscious' attention by casting it in a positive light.

And the subconscious responds by delivering on the positive interpretation, not the negative one.

Desire Versus Reality

Philosophers and achievers throughout history agree that if we continually transmit a positive thought to our subconscious minds, by repeatedly saying something aloud that reflects our desire, that desire will become reality.

More than a century ago the French philosopher Émile Coué flatly told people they would feel—and actually *be*—happier and more successful if they stood in front of a mirror and said out loud twice a day, "Every day, in every way, I'm getting better and better." A lot of people laughed at the idea, because they couldn't believe that something so simple, so effortless, could have so lasting and favorable an effect on human life.

But it's true: the constant repetition day after day of a positive thought, an affirmation, eventually takes root in your subconscious. It usually takes a minimum of three to four weeks for affirmations to bed themselves into your subconscious.

The same timetable applies to making and breaking habits of any kind. One or two weeks of persisting with a New Year's resolution isn't going to bring about the behavioral change it was intended to. But keep

Tiger laughs with Steve after chipping in for birdie at the 2005 PGA Championship at Baltusrol Golf Club in Springfield, New Jersey.

Tiger looks over the eighth green with Steve during round three of the 2005 U.S. Open at the Pinehurst Resort in North Carolina.

above: Steve and Tiger on the par-three 7th hole during the completion of the first round of the 2004 Dubai Desert Classic in the United Arab Emirates.

below: Tiger and Steve celebrate after Tiger defeated Chris DiMarco in a sudden-death playoff during the final round of the 2005 Masters at the Augusta National Golf Club in Georgia.

Tiger is congratulated by Steve after chipping in to save par on the 14th hole during the final round of the 2004 Memorial Tournament at Muirfield Village Golf Club in Dublin, Ohio.

right: The moment of inspiration: the young Steve Williams (right) discusses club selection with five-time British Open winner Peter Thomson at the New Zealand Open at Heretaunga in 1976. After this tournament, there was only one thing Steve ever wanted to be: the world's best caddy.

STEVE WILLIAMS

STEVE WILLIAMS

Among Steve's early clients was the English-born Scot Sandy Lyle, winner of the 1985 British Open and the 1988 U.S. Masters. Steve caddied for Lyle while waiting to get the Green Card that would allow him to work with Greg Norman in the United States as well as elsewhere, and helped Lyle gain credit for breaking the American dominance of the game.

left: Steve looks on sympathetically while Greg Norman, for whom he caddied for eight years, ponders the vagaries of the game. The relationship was so close it eventually became claustrophobic for both of them, leading to an amicable split. They remain close friends.

STEVE WILLIAMS

right: Another of Steve's European clients who helped bring an end to the American dominance of golf was Germany's Bernhard Langer, U.S. Masters champion in 1985 and 1993, and ten-time member of the European Ryder Cup team. Much of Steve's understanding of how to control the putting "yips" came from Langer's successful battle against this psychological handicap.

STEVE WILLIAMS

above: Steve added a few years to his actual age to get the job caddying for the Great White Shark, Australian Greg Norman. It was two years into their partnership before Norman accidentally found out Steve was distinctly younger than he had been led to believe. It's been a standing joke between them ever since.

below: A trio of the greats: (from left) Raymond Floyd, Steve and Arnold Palmer. Steve caddied for Floyd for 11 years, and was considering retiring when Tiger Woods tapped him on the shoulder.

Raymond Floyd had Steve on his bag when he became the first person to win both the PGA and the Champions (Seniors) tours in the same year. With Steve caddying for him, Floyd's ailing career suddenly burst back into life.

it up for a month or so and the new behavior becomes firmly established in place of the old.

Affirmations work by constantly reinforcing the changes you want to make in your life.

Entire religions are structured around affirmations—some call them prayers, some call them mantras. Affirmations are self-fulfilling prophecies. They can work with negative messages no less than with positive ones, but it's the positives that we're interested in here. The more the positive message is imprinted on your subconscious, the closer you get to the message becoming reality.

Outwardly the affirmation doesn't seem to change anything at first, but inwardly it'll be making its imprint on the subconscious. Within about 30 days you'll start to see the message expressing itself in your spontaneous thought patterns.

People usually live up to the expectations, good or bad, that other people have of them, but they always live up to the expectations they have of themselves. We are what we think we are. Change people's perceptions of themselves and you change the people.

When we repeat an affirmation over and over, we begin to expect to see changes in our personality and/or performance, and we begin to act like the person and/or performer we want to become. Because we've changed the perception of ourselves, we've changed our actual person.

It doesn't matter whether or not we believe in the power of affirmations, any more than it matters whether or not we believe in the power of gravity. If we use affirmations constantly we will experience change, no less than if we step off a cliff we will begin to fall.

We've only got to listen in on the conversations in the clubroom to observe the power of affirmations. There we'll find people who practice negative affirmations all the time, and most of us fall into the habit of it at least occasionally. We might hear a frustrated player say, "I can't strike the ball right," or "I can't get the flight I need," or "I'm forever hooking or slicing it." These are all negative affirmations—and, like positive ones, they're self-fulfilling prophecies. The more that people say they can't strike the ball right, the more they hook or slice it. The more they say they can't get the flight they need, the more foliage they knock out of the surrounding trees.

The more affirmations that we make, be they positive or negative, the more accurate they become.

The computer-brain is programmed to live up to the individual's expectations: if the individual says often enough that he can't do something, he'll prove himself absolutely right. But if he says often enough that he can do something, he'll likewise prove himself absolutely right.

So what's it to be? Positive or negative? Successful or unsuccessful? It's simply a matter of choice.

How to Write Affirmations

To create an affirmation, select an intermediate goal—short-term ones are too close to be usefully affected—and write it on a card in a way that suggests it's already been achieved. As with the master plan, stick it somewhere you'll come across it often, and read it—preferably out loud—whenever you do. As a minimum you'd need to do it at least half a dozen times a day.

This is a standard technique that professional motivators teach to salespeople. For example, you might have a car salesperson who has an intermediate goal of selling two cars a week throughout a year with the aim of making, say, $100,000. He would write his affirmation this way: "I am a top-line car salesperson. I sell over 100 cars a year and earn over $100,000." Sure, it works. That's why big corporations spend all that money on professional motivators to inspire their salespeople.

Having trouble with the way you strike the ball? Want to develop a swing where the ball gets away on line all the time? Write yourself an affirmation like this: "I strike the ball with machine-like precision. It feels as though the club is an extension of my body. My action is as smooth as silk."

Of course, at the time of writing it down, the statement isn't true. If it were true you wouldn't need to make it. But this doesn't make the statement a lie, because you're not trying to deceive anyone but your own subconscious. Rather, it's a projection into the future, a conditioning exercise. By constantly reinforcing the change you want to bring about, through a combination of goal-setting and repetition of the affirmation, the statement must inevitably come true.

One of the most famous affirmations in sports history was written by the coach of the seemingly invincible Notre Dame gridiron team that dominated college football in the 1940s and 1950s. Long before the American sports industry began to focus on the sports psychology, Notre

Dame coach Frank Leahy wrote out this affirmation in huge letters on the changing-room wall, and required every player to read it out loud before going onto the playing field: "When the going gets tough, the tough get going." It did and they were.

No less famous an affirmation was Muhammad Ali's self-fulfilling prophecy: "I am the greatest." At the time Ali started using his affirmation he was by no means the greatest. He was just a kid with quick hands and a chip on his shoulder because his 1960 Olympic heavyweight boxing gold medal brought him no respect in his hometown of Louisville, Kentucky. He went on to parlay his "I am the greatest" affirmation into three world professional championships over the next 15 years, despite losing several peak fighting years when banned by the sport's administrators for refusing to fight in the Vietnam War.

Affirmations are mottos or action statements. Writing them, reading them and seeing them every day imprints indelibly on the subconscious mind the attitudes needed for success.

At first it may be hard to adopt an affirmation you know just isn't true. You might be well aware that your swing is as lumpy as an old mattress, and it seems stupid to be standing in front of a mirror saying out loud how sweet it is. But constant repetition will commit your subconscious to working on it, not just getting closer to your true potential, but actually expanding the potential. Eventually the day arrives when you can look yourself squarely in the eye, say the words of your affirmation out loud, and know it is now true. That's when you create a new affirmation aimed at improving another aspect of your game.

By constantly repeating the affirmation, you establish the expectation of possessing a great swing, or whatever else you want, and because everyone lives up to the expectations they have of themselves, it's inevitable that the expectation becomes reality.

And Now the Big Picture . . .

Let's get back to our ambitious teenager, who's set himself the ultimate goal of winning a major. Let's say he's chosen an intermediate goal of taking out his local club's open title. Here's how he might write an affirmation to begin using, say, two months before the tournament, a time frame that gives the affirmation plenty of time to bed into the subconscious.

"I have won the club title," he writes. "I thrive on pressure, and play superbly against top opposition. I'm always relaxed, positive, and totally confident in my inner ability to outperform any opposition I meet."

At the time he writes the statement, the teenager might never have won anything beyond an age-group tournament. But he's got two months to make the statement a self-fulfilling prophecy.

Affirmations can be rigid and long-term—like Ali's "I am the greatest"—and used from the start of the campaign to the realization of the ultimate goal. But their more important application is in reaching intermediate goals, for which a new affirmation is written each time round. They can't be geared to a short-term goal because it takes a month or so for an affirmation to bed into your subconscious and start affecting your performance. With small adaptations, the same affirmation could be used for a succession of intermediate goals, but for variety's sake it's better to have a new affirmation for each one.

Either way, affirmations serve as a lighthouse in the darkness of the subconscious.

As a rule of thumb, the longer our teenager intends retaining essentially the same affirmation, the shorter and more generalized it should be. For intermediate goals, the affirmation can be longer and more specific. For our teenager with an ultimate goal of winning a major 10-20 years out, "I have won the Masters" is about as specific as he needs. By the time he makes the Masters field, if he's said it out loud and sincerely to his own face several times a day for all those years, he'll not only believe it, but in all probability it'll be about to come true.

To Recap

We've now put in place two of the three main mental tools required to play better golf simply by thinking about it. First we had the goal-setting—definitely the most important. Now we've got the affirmation—a secondary but no less vital tool. If we were to describe goal-setting as the horse, affirmations would be the saddle and bridle.

In the next chapter we'll introduce the jockey, the third of the core ingredients of performance enhancement by mind-training.

9

Visualization, Imagination and Creativity

Most golfers prepare for disaster. A good golfer prepares for success.
—Bob Toski

Visualization saved Raymond Floyd's career.

Back in 1989, at the age of 46, Floyd looked washed up. He had 21 PGA Tour victories behind him, including four majors (the PGA Championships of 1969 and 1982, the 1976 Masters and the 1986 U.S. Open). But by the end of the 1980s he had slumped to 145th on the money list with winnings of only $74,000.

At the time, I had recently stopped caddying for Greg Norman after our eight-year relationship had descended into mutual claustrophobia. We got on so well initially that I allowed myself to get too close to him, and eventually we both felt stifled by it. Getting that close to a player was a mistake I'll never make again.

I was quickly snapped up by Andy Bean, the flamboyant American from Georgia with 11 PGA Tour victories to his credit, his last two in 1986. But like Floyd, Bean was struggling with a form slump at a time when both these aging champions were setting their sights on a seamless shift to the Champions (Seniors) Tour when they turned 50 years of age. I was the caddy Bean wanted to take with him. But Floyd, a good friend of Greg Norman's, also began looking to me to help resurrect his flagging career.

It was a difficult choice to make, especially because Bean didn't want to lose me. But I decided to go with Floyd anyway, despite the fact that he was in a deeper and seemingly more intractable slump than Bean. The switch had more than a little to do with my continuing friendship with Norman: our personal relationship survived our professional split, which itself had been amicable. We remain close friends to this day. Whatever Norman's influence was in favor of Floyd, I still faced a choice between one struggling former champion and another. I made the switch because in the end Floyd convinced me that he had a better recovery plan than Bean.

And so it proved. I teamed up with Floyd, which helped precipitate a startling rejuvenation of his form, while Bean's went into further decline (Bean eventually joined the Seniors Tour in 2003, but despite having the season's low round of six-under 64 managed only one top-10 finish).

Raymond Floyd's end-of-the-'80s slump had much to do with his swing. It's famously unorthodox, cramped and uneven, and it had been blamed for his two previous slumps: between 1970 and 1975, and between 1979 and 1981—seven mid-career years when he never scored a single win on the PGA Tour. When I teamed up with him in 1989, he was still concentrating on trying to knock the lumps out of his swing, without much success.

Soon after my arrival, Floyd made the decision to forget about the vagaries of the swing itself and concentrate instead on doing the best he could with it. As part of his pre-stroke routine, he started forming a mental picture—visualizing—where he wanted the ball to go, rather than how the club was going to propel it there. With my help in feeding him the yardages and course information, and his use of a new graphite-shafted driver given to him by Japanese great Masashi "Jumbo" Ozaki, he produced a dramatic turnaround in his game. At the age of 47 he finished the regulation rounds of the 1990 Masters tied with the defending champion, Britain's Nick Faldo (British Open 1987, 1990; Masters 1989, 1990), the hottest player on the Tour at the time. Never mind that on the second hole of the playoff Floyd hooked his approach shot into the water hazard to the left of the green on Augusta's 455-yard par-four 11th: to get that close to a fifth major title 21 years after his first was nothing short of remarkable.

It was the visualization that did it.

From there, Floyd went on to 14 victories on the Seniors Tour over the next decade, crowning that achievement with his 1992 Doral-Ryder

Open victory—the first time anyone had won a PGA tournament in the same year he won on the Seniors Tour. It was a feat not equaled until 2003, when Craig Stadler (Masters 1982) won both the Ford Senior Players Championship and the PGA's BC Open in the very same year.

So what's the magic?

Thus far we've described conscious thought—the "person"—as something of a barrier to good golf. And for most players it is. Conscious thought tends to impose value judgments on the information from the senses being fed into the subconscious by the RAM, with the result that the subconscious sends confused and conflicting instructions to the body on how to execute the shot. So far we've addressed this problem by developing a mental mechanism (which we'll further refine later on) for switching conscious thought off throughout the minute or so when we address the ball and play the shot.

The switching-off principle still applies, but conscious thought has a wonderful upside that we can add to the equation being worked out by the subconscious. It's called imagination.

Through the imagination, conscious thought can create mind pictures that it can superimpose over the visions our eyes are seeing in real time. It's an extraordinary creative capability, the sort that sets the human brain apart from the computer which it otherwise resembles in so many respects. The computer can only respond to the data fed into it. It can't create. It can't imagine. It can't visualize.

The power to imagine, to visualize, is what will probably always distinguish the human brain from the computer. This puts into perspective the question of whether science will ever produce a computer guided robot that could play golf better than humans. It's a question that has logically arisen since world chess champion Garry Kasparov was beaten at his own game by a computer called Deep Blue in 1997.

In response to the surge in public interest that followed Deep Blue's world-shaking victory, the Robotics Institute at Carnegie Mellon University did a study into trends in computer development, to see when the processing power and memory capacity of cheap machines would match the general intellectual performance of humans. The university estimated such machines should be on the market sometime in the 2020s.

Should we be afraid of computers taking over the world—or worse: taking over golf? No.

Processing power and memory capacity are one thing. Imagination is quite another. Deep Blue didn't out-imagine Garry Kasparov. It simply out-remembered and out-processed him. An analogy to this might be the car industry, where computer-guided robots have taken over most of the work of building cars. But only a human could have imagined robots building cars in the first place. No machine, no computer, could conceive of such a development. The computer is, in the end, just a tool and, at the point where imagination enters the equation, it lacks any capability comparable to the human brain.

What visualization does is to put that uniquely human capability, the imagination, to work *for* us rather than against us. Instead of letting it mess up the immediate and environmental information being gathered by the senses and fed to the subconscious by the RAM, we're going to give it another job to do. We'll still need that switching mechanism, but from now on it won't be so much a case of switching the conscious mind off as switching it into a different mode—a creative one. We're going to employ it in a positive rather than a negative or passive way.

We've already seen that it's the nature of the imagination to deal with things in either the past or the future. We've seen that without imagination we'd have no desires, no dreams to fulfill. Without imagination we couldn't enjoy success, couldn't experience disappointment. But if we use it in a positive fashion we can get it to create pictures of the future, and impose those on the present. We need to employ the imagination like a video or movie camera, to demonstrate to the subconscious, in perfect detail and vivid color, exactly what the perfect golf shot looks like every time we address the ball.

A Picture Is Worth . . .

In the last chapter we looked at affirmations, such as, "I have a swing that's smooth as silk." Just saying that out loud will eventually bed it into the subconscious, but our brains react far faster to pictures than to words. The saying "A picture is worth a thousand words" could not be more apt than when applied to the imagination's capacity to influence the subconscious in real time, in the now. Affirmations take a month to fully penetrate the subconscious. Visualization—the imagination—penetrates immediately.

Using visualization in conjunction with affirmations makes our imagination work positively for us. Picturing and feeling the perfect swing in our imagination, and at the same time affirming to ourselves that we're performing it as smoothly as silk, can bring about only one result: we develop a swing that's as smooth as silk. It takes us into another dimension of data-collecting to feed the subconscious, by employing as many of the five senses as we can: not only do we see the shot we're about to make but, in our imagination, we can also feel, taste, touch and smell it.

Yes, smell it.

How can you smell the perfect golf shot? Simply by using the imagination to connect the positive vibes from our favorite smells—fresh flowers, old leather, steak on the grill—with the delicious satisfaction of getting the ball to go precisely where we want it to. The principle, equally applicable to taste, is the basic one with which we began our analysis of the mind game of golf, namely the need to fill the subconscious with accurate and uncluttered data to help it formulate the actual shot.

Telling our gullible, non-judgmental subconscious to connect the execution of the forthcoming shot with the satisfaction generated by our favorite smells, tastes and sounds reinforces the positive messages our imagination is sending it about the flight of the ball and the feel of the swing. It's all a matter of bombarding the subconscious with positive images uncluttered by value judgments.

The subconscious can't distinguish between the relevance of what the eyes are seeing and the irrelevance of smells and tastes and sounds. All it can do is incorporate these positive concepts, stored in the hard-disk memory files, into the shot it's formulating. Positive messages generate happy outcomes.

Employing visualization and positive vibes from the other senses alongside affirmation may or may not speed up the process of bedding affirmations into the subconscious. But taking this multi-faceted approach to schooling the subconscious will unquestionably bed the desired behaviors in place more deeply and permanently than would be possible using affirmations or visualization alone.

It's like the difference between writing "Mom" on your shoulder with a felt pen (spoken affirmations alone), and getting a tattoo artist to do it (affirmations, visualization and the other sensory perceptions combined).

The Mind's Eye

To the legion of golfers who model themselves on him, Tiger Woods holds the patent on the classic, perfect swing—that silken, whippy action that concentrates so much energy in the clubhead at the point of contact with the ball. For anyone aspiring to emulate it, the trick is to put yourself in Tiger's picture, to see yourself in your mind's eye, in your imagination, swinging that club with the same grace and power.

"To see" is the operative term. The imagination gives us the capacity to create a vision that doesn't exist, and the more efficiently we can exercise the imagination through the medium of the senses, the more powerful the images that will be sent to the subconscious.

See with your mind's eye the oiled Woods action—only it's you in the picture: your face, your shape; it's you feeling that club in your hands, you addressing that ball.

With practice you become fluent in the mental language of forming clear, precise pictures—videos of the imagination—that complement the messages the subconscious has been getting from the affirmations. The greater the fluency of this language of the imagination, the sooner the affirmative goal becomes reality.

It's an exercise in describing to the subconscious what you, the conscious "person," want to see happen, by supplying it with clear, vibrant pictures of the goal achieved. Once the subconscious has got the picture—preferably enhanced by other imaginary sensations—and has begun to store the repeatable bits away on the hard drive as well as incorporating them into the ensuing shot, it's fully primed to deliver a performance that reflects the individual's full potential.

Informing the Future

The same affirmation-to-achievement process can be applied usefully to the future tournament or ultimate goal, no less than to the next shot to be played in the present. Our ambitious teenager can see himself playing the big match, can become a spectator to his own moment of triumph. In his mind's eye he sees how cool, calm, relaxed and confident he looks as he steps up to the first tee in his long-anticipated major. He can see, feel, taste, hear and touch the positive vibes he's giving off to his opponents. His aim is to make that picture so clear, so precise and believable, that his subconscious accepts it as being as real as if it were happening right then and there.

That's when it starts to become real.

This is the essence of that magic ingredient that the top golfers are always talking about: self-belief. It's not the blind belief of the religious or political fundamentalist. Instead it's an informed belief based on the huge database on the hard drive of the subconscious—a database created *by* ourselves, *for* ourselves.

Marry goal-setting and affirmation programs to the imagination's extraordinary power to visualize creatively, and you've started a sequence of changes in the subconscious that guarantees success.

The goal seen becomes the goal believed becomes the goal achieved.

To inform his future this way, our ambitious teenager will plan regular sessions where he gets away somewhere by himself, either in a comfy chair or stretched out on his bed. He starts off by reading his affirmation out loud, with his eyes open. The trick in this is to prime the subconscious by sending it signals through at least one of the physical senses. Reading the affirmation engages sight, speaking it out loud engages hearing. If he could touch, smell or taste his affirmation as well, so much the better.

Now he closes his eyes and projects his imagination to the moment of achieving his goal. He sees himself walking up the 18th at Augusta to where his 300-yard-plus drive has finished up on the fairway, close to those famous trees on the right, well away from those two murderous bunkers on the left, and with a clear iron shot between the two front bunkers that guard the green. He feels the iron in his hand; smells the scent of the Georgia spring; savors the taste of impending victory; hears the hushing of the crowd; sees the pin as clearly as if it were just meters away; sees too the old colonial-style clubhouse beyond it with the Stars and Stripes flying at the top of the flagpole, and the green flag of the National Golf Club fluttering below it. His swing is like silk. The crowd roars. He's on the green, inches from the hole.

He putts.

He wins.

He plays this video of his ultimate achievement through his head twice a day with every variation in detail he can think of. He doesn't have to spend more than five minutes each session on it, but it becomes both the spur to keep him focused on his ultimate goal, and the painkiller when he encounters the inevitable frustrations and disappointments.

Play-by-Play Use of Creative Visualization

But let's come back to the immediate, to that next shot he's about to play. Take the example of Jack Nicklaus, the Golden Bear, still the greatest golfer in history with 18 majors to his credit (British Open 1966, 1970 and 1978; U.S. Open 1962, 1967, 1972 and 1980; Masters 1962, 1965, 1966, 1972, 1975 and 1986; PGA 1962, 1971, 1973, 1975 and 1980). Nicklaus always said that, before he swung the club, he formed a picture in his mind of the shot he was going to play. He made the picture vibrant, packed with as much detail as he could get into it: the weather, the color of the sky, the shapes of the trees. When playing, say, an iron to the green, he took his stance, then pictured the ball rising into the sky, hovering over the green, then coming down and landing next to the pin. The clearer and more precise the picture was, the better he knew the shot would be.

Using Nicklaus' experience as a template, we can create a pre-shot visualization routine that excludes the negative value judgments to which the conscious "person" is prone—a routine in which the imagination feeds the subconscious with pictures of where the ball must end up and the trajectory it must take to get there. We'll actually have three separate visualizations, organized in the reverse order to the actual shot.

Let's join our player after he's caught up with his ball following his tee shot on a par four, when he's facing an iron shot to the green. Before he addresses the ball he shuts off his conscious mind and allows his senses to gather every bit of information they can about the situation. His caddy, assuming he has one, will have given him the yardages and the wind direction and force. Otherwise it's up to his senses and his local knowledge to figure them out as precisely as he can. He gives his senses 15–20 seconds to absorb all this data, from the lie of the ball to the distance it has to travel, to the obstacles it has to avoid, to the wind it has to contend with. He lets his RAM transfer this immediate environmental data to his subconscious without conscious comment or value judgment.

Now he steps up for his practice swing and commences the first of three visualization exercises. In this first one he sees the ball landing on the green and trickling towards the hole. He performs this visualization with his eyes open. With practice, he'll "see" a virtual ball imposed on his real-time vision in much the way that television producers impose graphics on a real-time screen.

With the picture of the target point fixed in his mind's eye, he executes his practice swing to prime his subconscious for the upcoming stroke, and the subconscious instantly collects all the relevant swing files from its hard-disk memory.

Now the player addresses the ball and commences the second visualization. In this one he sees the trajectory the ball must take to the target point on the green. He superimposes this trajectory, as graphically as his imagination will allow him, onto his real-time view of the ball's flight path. Greg Norman had a variation on this exercise, putting special emphasis in his visualization on the height of the ball at the peak of its trajectory. Norman fixed the height in relation to nearby trees or some feature in the background, and found it an aid to imprinting the ball's flight path in his subconscious.

Whether or not our ambitious teenager has added this variation to his routine, he allows a few seconds for this combined real-and-imaginary vision to burn itself into his subconscious as he makes the final adjustments to his footing and sets the clubhead behind the ball.

Now he enters his third and final visualization, and in some respects it's the easiest of the three because all the information he needs is right there in front of him. He has the clubhead positioned almost up against the ball, in exactly the spot he wants the clubface to be in when they make contact. He allows a few seconds for this picture to burn itself into his imagination so that it stays there after he withdraws the clubhead for the backswing.

Even when the clubhead has been withdrawn outside his range of vision he's still seeing it frozen in his mind's eye at that millisecond when it makes contact with the ball. He's so focused on that picture that he's not aware of anything else—not the club departing, not his backswing, not his swing, not the club returning, not the follow-through: nothing but that picture of the clubhead caught, as if by a high-speed freeze-frame camera, at the point of impact.

Then suddenly his follow-through drags his head up and around. The vision is broken and the ball is gone. He catches up and follows it with his eyes, sucking in every last detail of its flight so that any variation between the visualized and the actual trajectory registers on the sub-conscious as comparative information to be stored in the hard-disk memory files.

That is the shot-making cycle. Now the imaginative computer shuts down and the human being takes over again until it's ready to repeat the whole exercise for the next shot. Follow this routine on every shot you make, regardless of the club, and you're doing it the way the pros do it.

To recap: there are three separate visualizations. The first is of the ball landing on the green and rolling towards the hole. The second is of the ball's trajectory in flight. The third and final one is of the clubhead at the point of impact on the ball—that is, right where it sits before the backswing begins.

The reason for doing these visualizations in reverse real-time order—that is, the landing first, the trajectory second and the impact of club on ball last—is because all the outputs formulated by the subconscious are concentrated into the instant of the clubhead's impact on the ball. Once the ball's in flight, there's nothing the subconscious can do about it. The impact visualization is thus the most important of the three, so needs to be kept freshest in the subconscious.

The Putting Variation

The only variation to the routine is for putting. On the green only two visualizations are needed because the target and trajectory visualizations can be rolled into one: that of the ball rolling towards and dropping into the cup. This leaves just the impact visualization to immediately precede the actual putt.

The golfer first performs the combined target/trajectory visualization while he's surveying the run to the hole, before he actually steps up to make the putt. Standing well back with the ball between him and the hole, the player visualizes its trail to the cup at the same time as his senses take in all the variables—the surface and speed of the green, the wind, the humps and hollows—that might affect the way it rolls. He might repeat the exercise from the other side of the green, just to improve the quality of data the RAM is feeding into his subconscious.

When he stands up to the ball for his practice putting action, he repeats the first visualization of it rolling to the hole along the same line he pictured when he was standing back from it.

Finally, as he addresses the ball, his visualization switches to the moment of impact of the putter on the ball. His priority now is to get the ball rolling along the track he has just visualized and, as with the full-swing strokes, this is dependent above all on the geometry of the club-head at the point of impact. To achieve this he takes one last look along the ball's intended trail and keeps as much of it in his line of vision as he can. But the prime focus of his vision and visualization alike is the point of impact.

It's vital that, at the point of impact, the putter-head is at right angles to both the surface of the green in one plane, and the intended track of the ball in the other. Sure, it helps if the hole is visible out of the corner of the player's eye, but the hole itself becomes irrelevant to the putting action once the correct track to it has been visualized and the putter-head is precisely square on.

Finally, still visualizing the perfect geometry between clubhead, ball and track, and keeping his eyes fixed on the point of impact, the golfer makes the putt.

Making It Stick

Goal-setting, affirmation and visualization are the key components of the mind game of successful golf. But what we need to look at now are techniques for making the mind as receptive as it can possibly be to this three-pronged strategy. The mind is at its most receptive when it is relaxed.

So now let's spend a little time finding out *how* to relax.

10

Relaxation Techniques

Relax? How can anybody relax and play golf? You have to grip the club, don't you?

—Ben Hogan

Just seconds before, he might have erupted into gesticulating Spanish in one of his famous outbursts at his caddy—especially if the caddy happened to be one of his brothers, Vicente or Manuel—but Severiano Ballesteros (British Open 1979, 1984 and 1988; Masters 1980 and 1983) knew how to relax and recover his composure on the course. He had a unique way of doing it. He'd stop waving his arms, and instead fold them while he took in a deep, deep breath. Then he'd press his hands hard against the bottom of his ribcage. It would have been more than a little painful, but he'd hold this posture for 10–20 seconds. The he'd let go and exhale, and he'd be restored to the Seve everyone knew, the inspiring competitor—his leadership of European Ryder Cup teams is legendary—and one of the game's greatest players.

Greg Norman had a different method of relaxing, which he'd employ before teeing off in every tournament he played. He'd close his eyes, take a deep breath, and tilt his head as far as he could from side to side a few times, as if trying to get his ears to touch his shoulders. Then he'd straighten up, exhale slowly, and finally open his eyes again.

Most of the pros have some routine or other for releasing tension between holes or shots, and knowing when and how to help has been one of the features of my caddying. I'm a good conversationalist, and these days the television cameras often catch Tiger Woods and me deep in discussion as we stalk the fairways.

We talk about lots of things, but it's usually sports—any sport, that is, except golf. Sometimes I will regale Tiger with stories from my rugby-playing days, and updates on how my beloved All Blacks are faring on the world stage. Sometimes it's cars and dirt-track racing. Frequently we joke about basketball: Tiger, a close friend of NBA legend Michael Jordan, is a fan of his hometown Florida team the Orlando Magic, while as a part-time Oregon resident, I support the Portland Trailblazers. In baseball Tiger likes the Los Angeles Dodgers; while I root for the Chicago Cubs, in part because my former boss Raymond Floyd tried out for them when he was younger. Floyd still retains a locker in their clubhouse.

Whatever the on-course relaxation routine, it's vital for a player to deliberately break his concentration between shots.

It would be absolutely exhausting, if not mentally impossible, to maintain full concentration throughout the four hours or so it takes to play a round of golf. You've got to take your mind off the game between shots.

The ideal state of mind on the course is to be loose and relaxed. You've got to conserve your mental energies by minimizing the amount of time that you're at full concentration. If you're thinking about the next shot from the moment you leave the tee until you catch up with your ball, you're expending too much of the mind's energy. As a caddy, I want to keep my player loose and relaxed throughout the time he doesn't need to focus.

Once the mind gets weary, the body gets weary.

As a former international schoolboy rugby player, I know as well as anyone the need for players in all sports to approach their game with a relaxed and "loose" mind. This applies to a frenetic and violent sport like rugby just as much to a sedate and measured one like golf. You could hardly find two sports less alike: one a team sport, the other an individual one; one an almost non-stop running and body-contact exercise, the other a gently paced affair in which, at least theoretically, the player doesn't need to have any physical or emotional contact with the competition. But in both cases the players' minds and muscles need to be relaxed, and mental tension dissipated, for the various skills to be executed to maximum effect.

Players also have to develop the capacity to relax before, during and after competition. Like the physical techniques involved in both sports, relaxation is an acquired skill that has little to do with letting your hair down afterwards. Certainly in golf the relaxation skill factor required for top competition has ballooned over the last few decades, no doubt in direct proportion to the amounts of prize money on offer.

A Whole New Skill Set

When the Royal and Ancient Golf Club of St. Andrew's held a millennial dinner to honor former champions, Sam Snead (Masters champion 1949, 1952 and 1954; U.S. Open 1946; PGA 1942, 1949 and 1951) remarked that the idea of relaxation for players of his generation was to "party until late and then play hung-over." To which Tiger Woods was heard to respond, "That doesn't work any more."

Relaxation has taken on a whole new meaning since the days when it was synonymous with letting your hair down. These days it takes practice, not alcohol.

Relaxation is not a matter of sitting around doing nothing, or overworking the bar staff at the 19th. True relaxation is an exercise, as deliberate and performance-oriented as goal-setting, reciting affirmations, honing your swing on the driving range or polishing your putting on the practice green.

Relaxation is learned behavior. It doesn't necessarily come naturally, even for such laid-back characters as Ernie Els and Fred Couples. Yet the ability to stay relaxed throughout the execution of every shot is crucial to the golfer.

Almost as important is the ability to relax between shots, and both before and after a game. Combining relaxation exercises on and off the golf course with affirmation and visualization exercises creates the optimum environment for developing all these mental skills. Visualization and affirmation become most effective if the body is relaxed and the mind is quiet and uncluttered, allowing it to absorb mental pictures without distraction.

Physical relaxation might be easier to achieve on a sofa in the living room at home than out on the golf course in the middle of a game, but even in a relatively low-physical-input game like golf, the body, no less than the mind, needs to use the breaks between shots to recover from its previous exertions. The body recovers fastest when it's most relaxed.

Continuous practice of relaxation techniques results in two positive psychological changes. The first is muscular, the second to do with brainwave patterns. Let's look at them in turn.

Muscular Control

The key to controlling the muscular tension that builds up before and during a game is breathing. Breathing patterns change with our emotional state. If we're angry, our breathing accelerates to shallow inhalations and short, sharp exhalations. If we're sad or sobbing, inhaling is fitful and jerky, while exhaling is weak and uneven. Tiredness makes us yawn; fear makes us hold our breath.

It follows that, since breathing patterns reflect our emotional state, changing our breathing can change the way we feel.

As physical tiredness catches up with us during a game—and a four-hour walk is inevitably tiring, no matter how young you are—deep, relaxed breathing will accelerate recovery (and, incidentally, make you feel less tired than you actually are). Our ambitious teenager and our club hack alike need to relax mentally to be able to exercise awareness during the pauses between shots, and they need to relax physically to speed up their recovery. Proper breathing, as a conscious exercise, will help with both.

The way to breathe properly is through the diaphragm, the sheet of muscle that separates the chest cavity from the abdomen. Normal breathing is shallow, and is especially so when you're trying to repay the oxygen debt that comes from walking uphill carrying a 45 pound bag of golf clubs and attendant equipment and supplies, like I do for a living. Diaphragm breathing involves getting the lungs to fill from the bottom up.

In deep diaphragm breathing, you feel the lower ribcage expand first, then the chest, until the lungs are filled to capacity. It's a case of sucking in air from the bottom of the lungs up. Suck in as much air as can be comfortably accommodated, allowing the lungs the opportunity to extract as much oxygen out of it as they can, and the heart to pump it through the bloodstream to where the oxygen shortage is greatest (usually in the legs).

Having felt his stomach draw down and out until he can inhale no more, our golfer expels the air quickly through his mouth until his lungs are empty and it feels as if his stomach is sticking to his ribcage. As he breathes out, his stomach draws up and in, and he feels—that is, he makes himself consciously aware of—all the tension floating out with the air. Then he sucks in the next lungful.

During the off-the-course relaxation breathing, to prepare for or to accompany his affirmation and visualization exercises, our golfer breathes more slowly and deliberately than when he's trying to make up the oxygen debt after a brisk uphill walk during a game. Again he's conscious of filling his lungs from the bottom up. He breathes in through his nose (something he can't do so well under heavy oxygen debt) and slowly out through his mouth. When his breathing has settled into a deep, slow pattern, and he's stretched out comfortably in a chair or on a bed, he can start the affirmation and visualization exercises, confident that his carefully induced state of relaxation will ensure the images he's creating in his imagination imprint themselves firmly on the subconscious.

This sort of nasal-oral breathing is also employed on the golf course once the oxygen debt, built up by the exercise of walking to the ball, has been repaid. It's called deep aerobic breathing (as distinct from anaerobic breathing, which is what you do when you're in oxygen debt) and is a standard practice among pro-golfers, as exemplified by the Seve Ballesteros and Greg Norman routines.

There are all sorts of variations on the aerobic breathing that pro-golfers introduce to their pre-shot routines. Some players wiggle their arms, some do neck exercises, and some even do a little dance to loosen up during their aerobic breathing. It's important, though, to clear up the oxygen debt—that is, to wait until you've stopped puffing after the exertion of walking to the tee or the ball—before beginning the aerobic breathing as part of the pre-shot routine.

I've had a considerable impact on this aspect of Tiger Woods' game. From my rugby days I learned the value of overall physical fitness to the golfer, and passed it on to Tiger by way of example. I have always run at least five miles a day six days a week, and fitted in at least one 1100-yard swim, as part of my personal fitness regime. Within a year after we teamed up, Tiger had adopted the daily run as an integral part of his own preparation.

This flies in the face of the perception that golf provides sufficient physical training for golfers, especially when they're as young and lean as Tiger. I'm adamant that no one in any field of endeavor, physical or otherwise, can perform to their optimum without attaining some measure of heightened cardiovascular fitness. I was indirectly exposed to such ideas as a youth at school by fellow New Zealander Arthur Lydiard, one of the great middle- and long-distance running coaches of the era. Lydiard guided the likes of Peter Snell (Olympic 800 m gold medallist in 1960, and 800 m and 1500 m in 1964; world 800 m, 1500 m, half-mile and mile record-holder, among others) and Murray Halberg (Olympic gold medallist 5000 m 1960; world record-holder 5000 m). Lydiard pioneered the principle of slow long-distance aerobic running—"Train, don't strain," was his motto—of 100 miles a week or more as the prerequisite for optimum performance on the rugby field, no less than on the running track. His ideas gained wide currency in New Zealand in the late 1960s and early 1970s, and I can attest to their effectiveness today not only for rugby but for golf as well.

Incidentally, it was Tiger Woods who introduced me to the concept of weight training, something that Arthur Lydiard tended to regard as unnecessary to a runner. But as bag-man to the best, I feel my overall fitness has been helped significantly by adding weightlifting to my regular exercise routine.

Another point about breathing and the golfer's pre-shot exercises is that the routine should be identical from shot to shot. Variations in routine require imaginative input, at a time when the golfer should be concentrating all his imaginative powers on visualization. He should ritualize his pre-shot routine so he never has to waste his mental energies on introducing new concepts to it.

An exercise that shows the importance of muscular relaxation is to take two small objects of similar size but different weight—say, an apple and an orange—and then to tense the muscles in the arm and hand before picking them up one after the other, and grasping them fairly firmly. See if you can tell the difference in weight.

Now repeat the exercise, but this time first do the aerobic diaphragm-breathing exercise described earlier. As you breathe out, imagine all the tension flowing down your arm and out of your hands through your fingertips, until you're completely relaxed. Now pick up each object gently and sense the difference in weight.

Notice the difference? Moral of the story: you'll find it a lot easier to judge, say, driving weight and distance—that is, "feel"—when your muscles are loose and flexible. Tension in the muscles distorts the information being sent to the subconscious. The relaxed golfer can trust his subconscious to add, say, that fraction of weight to a drive that's at the end of his comfortable (75 percent effort) range, without pulling or slic-ing it. The tense golfer consciously tries to add the weight but, since try-ing necessarily involves tension, he's not giving his subconscious the chance to make the necessary adjustment the way it does best: sponta-neously.

Brain-Wave Control

The second relaxation principle that produces psychological benefits is brain-wave control. Measurements of the brain-wave rhythms in young children learning complex skills, like walking and talking, shows a much slower pattern than in adults. As we age, these rhythms accelerate steadi-ly, expanding the human sensory capacity to absorb and process an ever-increasing range of sights, feelings, tastes, sounds and smells. Adults tend to lose the ability to concentrate on a single event the way they could as a child, or to learn quickly from it, and this phenomenon is con-nected with the speeding up of the brain-wave rhythms.

The toddler operates at what is called alpha level, comprising eight to 13 brain-wave cycles a second. The adult is at beta level, which varies from 14–40 cycles a second. Excitement, tension and fear cause brain-waves to speed towards the top end of those scales. We can surmise from this that the slower the brain-wave rhythm, the better we concentrate. A baby can focus on one activity to the exclusion of everything else, and it's this level of intensely focused concentration that enables it to learn so rapidly.

As the maturing child begins to be affected by the sensory bom-bardment of modern living, brain-waves move from alpha to beta rhythm, and its ability to concentrate diminishes.

It's a bit like the reception on a single-channel television set: when just the one signal is coming through, the picture is clear and detailed. Multiply the signals and we begin to get ghosting and interference. The picture becomes fuzzy and scrambled because the television set can't isolate one message from the many its aerial is picking up.

As babies we all had this capacity to concentrate intently, and there's no reason for us to resign ourselves to the snowballing loss of it with age. In fact, we can get it back. All we have to do is develop the skill of slow-ing our brain-wave patterns down to alpha levels, and this is where relax-ation techniques, practiced off the golf course, come into play.

Twice-daily practice in relaxation will improve our ability to concentrate, and will also make affirmation and visualization more effective. Relaxation lets us clear out the interference and stress caused by sensory bombardment, so our minds can absorb, without distraction, pictures of our goals.

As a bonus, relaxation will also lower the blood pressure and minimize the effects of stress—it's like having an annual holiday twice a day.

There's a range of choices available to the golfer who wants to create a favorable mental environment in which to school his subconscious to produce better golf shots. Hypnosis—either self, or induced by a clinical hypnotist—is one. Here are a few others:

BREATHING MEDITATION

The technique of breathing meditation expands the concept of diaphragm breathing described earlier. As in all off-course relaxation techniques, it should be practiced in a place where there's no danger of being disturbed for the 20 minutes the exercise routine takes. The best times to do it are on getting up in the morning, and before the evening meal. The routine is additional to the off-course affirmation and visualization routines described in earlier chapters.

Our golfer sits in a comfortable chair with both feet on the floor, his back straight and his hands resting palm up in his lap. He starts with the deep diaphragm breathing exercise. He does it three times, and as he exhales he visualizes all the tension flowing out of his body through his fingertips.

That done, he focuses entirely on his breathing. He makes himself aware of the air flowing in through his nose, feeling it fill his diaphragm, then his chest. As he breathes out, he is aware of the air traveling through his chest, throat and mouth. He doesn't consciously try to change the rhythm of his breathing: he's just aware of the flow. If other thoughts drift into his head, he doesn't fight to get rid of them. Rather, once he realizes they've intruded, he gently switches his attention away from them and back to his breathing.

Gradually a sense of relaxation sets in, along with a feeling of warmth that spreads throughout the body, often accompanied by a tingling sensation in the fingers and toes. After 15 minutes of this the body is permeated with a sense of relaxed well-being, and the subconscious is primed to receive data directly from the conscious mind. Now is the time for the golfer to visualize his affirmations, letting his imagination dwell on the satisfaction of realizing the goals they represent.

With practice it becomes a most refreshing exercise: 20 minutes of it and he'll feel like he's had a whole night's sleep.

TRANSCENDENTAL MEDITATION

It's difficult to teach the technique of transcendental meditation (TM) in a book. Like the associated practice of yoga, it's best learned individually from a trained teacher. It's not within the scope of this book to explain how the technique works but, because more and more sportspeople are taking it up, it may help to dispel some of the misconceptions about it that arose during the 1960s, when it suffered in Western societies from associations with the flower-power drug culture.

TM involves the repetition of a sound—called a mantra, and given to you by the teacher—made or spoken under the breath. The sound is simple and has no meaning or significance to the meditator, but concentrating on it eventually takes his mind to an altered state of consciousness, to something akin to pure awareness, where his brain-wave patterns and breathing slow down to such an extent that he enters a state of blissful relaxation.

He remains wide awake and totally aware of his surroundings, but has transcended—that is, escaped the confines of—conscious thought.

It's the nature of both the consciousness and the subconscious to prefer the more pleasurable of two alternatives. For example, if our subject was reading, and his favorite song came on the radio, his attention would switch to the music because effortless listening is more pleasurable than the effort of reading. In the same way, by concentrating on the mantra or meaningless sound, the subject's consciousness gradually switches, of its own accord, into the more pleasurable state of consciousness he used to experience as a child. It's in this state that he can most effectively transmit positive ideas to his subconscious.

TM is widely touted as a good means of dissolving stress. It may not work for everybody, but there's no shortage of those who swear by it, including many who were skeptical about it to begin with.

The main misconceptions about TM are that it's a belief system, or a religion, or something you can connect to only with the aid of hallucinogenic drugs. It's none of these things. Instead it's a technique practiced by people in many countries, from all walks of life and with widely differing religions—or none at all.

The effects are claimed to be cumulative: the more you practice TM, the less stress you feel in your daily life.

Meditation, transcendental or otherwise, works by inducing an awareness, an alpha brain-wave state, where the subconscious is at its most receptive for its daily dosages of affirmation and visualization. It works like the recharging of batteries in an appliance: it not only helps improve the subject's concentration on the sports field, but contributes to living relatively stress-free in the modern pressure-cooker society.

AUTOGENIC TRAINING

Another less exotic exercise done twice daily in 20-minute spells is autogenic training. This one can be learned from books but, until the instructions are learned by heart, the subject might have to have someone read them out as he goes through them. Alternatively, he could record them and play them back until he's memorized them and can repeat them silently to himself. Autogenic training exercises are also available commercially on cassette and CD.

The subject begins his autogenic training session by lying down on his back on a bed or the floor with a firm pillow supporting his head. His clothing should be loose and comfortable. He closes his eyes and breathes in deeply through his diaphragm, imagining, in as detailed and precise a way as he possibly can, that the weight of his body is pushing down on the mattress or carpet. At the same time he imagines that the bed or floor is pushing up.

He keeps this up for a few minutes, then switches his awareness to his feet, imagining them to be warm and heavy. He "feels" his skin and bones getting heavier and warmer.

Next he "feels" the heat and weight starting to spread up his legs and into his calf muscles. From there he lets the sensation move successively up through his thigh muscles and buttocks, lower back, stomach, chest and shoulders. After that he feels this heaviness and warmth, sometimes accompanied by pleasant tingling sensations, consuming his whole body, before traveling down his arms to exit his body through the fingertips.

With all that tension gone, he switches the sensation of weight and warmth to his head. He also starts to "feel" a cool breeze fan his forehead, which becomes progressively cooler, even as the rest of his body remains heavy and warm.

He's now in a state of deep relaxation. His skin tingles as healing energy flows through it, revitalizing both his physical and mental systems. He imagines himself floating on warm, fluffy clouds, rising as he breathes in, sinking down into their warmth as he breathes out.

He's conscious of how calm and peaceful he feels. He visualizes feeling this way when he's out on the course playing golf: relaxed, calm—even graceful. He tells himself, convinces his subconscious, that he can enter this state whenever he likes.

Now he takes three deep breaths, feeling the energy flow in as he inhales, and tension leaving as he exhales. Finally, he opens his eyes and sits up, stretching like a cat after a sleep.

Now he's ready for anything.

When first starting these exercises our golfer may feel a bit awkward or self-conscious, but that'll pass as the benefits flow in. Once he's comfortable with one of these relaxation techniques, he'll find he's in company with an army of top athletes—not just golfers—who swear by them.

All the techniques described so far—goal-setting, affirmation, creative visualization and relaxation—improve both the golfer's game and his attitude to it. Not only will he begin to experience unprecedented success but, perhaps more importantly, he'll start to get even greater enjoyment out of it.

This combination of mental-training systems is designed to lead our golfer to what the sports psychologists these days call the "peak experience"—the one that reveals what his potential really is. It's the benchmark by which he will rate all future performances.

11

Anchoring, Temperament and the Meaning of "Feel"

Always throw your clubs ahead of you. That way you don't waste energy going back to pick them up.

—"Terrible" Tommy Bolt

He was to golf what John McEnroe once was to tennis: a notoriously tempestuous character who raged against mistakes and misfortune as if the whole world was against him. Tommy Bolt—"Thunderbolt" was but one of the nicknames he attracted—won the 1958 U.S. Open, and came close to adding the 1971 PGA to his titles when he was 53 years old, but his tantrums were a sight to see. Bolt had a great swing but his putter tended to let him down, and in the U.S. Open at Cherry Hills in 1960 he punished it by heaving it into a lake, leading to a standing joke that a new challenge faced golf-equipment manufacturers: to make clubs that could float.

Despite it all—or, more likely, because of it all—Tommy Bolt was a crowd favorite whose sayings, like the one quoted above, have become entrenched in golfing lore. "Never," he once said, "break your putter and your driver in the same round, or you're dead." Other examples of his wisdom include, "Putting allows the touchy golfer two to four opportunities to blow a gasket in the short space of two to forty feet" and, "Golf is good for your soul: you get so mad at yourself you forget to hate your enemies."

Bolt racked up 15 PGA Tour victories but he, his detractors and admirers alike, suspected he would have won more if only he could have kept his temper under control. The prevailing view of Tommy was that if he got out of the wrong side of the bed in the morning, his putter would be swimming with the fish by the afternoon.

It's true: the mood a person wakes up in tends to dominate the way they operate for the rest of the day. Start off in a bad mood, and everything that happens afterwards tends to reinforce that negative outlook. Bad temper creates bad luck, arguments and disagreements—even aches and pains. Frustration on the golf course boils over into bad language and club-slinging, which only make matters worse.

Nobody can help waking up in a bad frame of mind: the subconscious gets up to all sorts of tricks while the conscious is asleep, and our mood tends to reflect whatever it was we were dreaming about at the time we woke. The subconscious can never be switched off because, if it were, our life-support systems—breathing, heartbeat, metabolism—would cease to function too.

The subconscious never needs the recovery period that sleep gives to the conscious mind and body. It works away constantly while we sleep, producing an endless succession of images and scenarios in the form of dreams. It doesn't matter whether we remember our dreams or not when we return to consciousness: we all have them all the time we're asleep—as well as for much of the time we're awake.

It might be called the Tommy Bolt rule of thumb: wake from a bad dream and expect to have a lousy day.

Of course everything we experience during the day is just that—an experience—with no logical connection to the night dreams that preceded it. Our day's experiences are inherently neither good nor bad, neither happy nor sad. It's our reaction to them that makes the difference. The bad mood that is the legacy of a bad dream becomes a succession of bad experiences only if we let it. It's our conscious attitude—that is, the positive or negative spin we put on the mood—that determines whether we feel the day's experiences are good or bad. We can control the way we feel about a conscious experience, regardless of what the subconscious got up to during the night.

And we can do it in advance. By using a technique called "anchoring," we can arrest negative reactions to given experiences and replace them with positive ones.

The Conscious Mind's Ignition Switch

This same technique of anchoring also provides us with the ignition key to the entire mind-training system and structure described in this book. In earlier chapters I talked about the need to take each stroke on the golf course in complete isolation from the ones that preceded it, and the ones to follow. I talked about the essence of this strategy being a mental switching mechanism: just before he addresses the ball, the golfer switches his conscious mind off and leaves the execution of the shot entirely up to the subconscious. On completion of the shot, the consciousness is switched back on again.

As a caddy, I help my golfer through these constant transitions by adding his yardages and associated information to the data the golfer is collecting for himself, and delivering to his subconscious by way of his awareness. Then I back off, and the golfer is left to switch his conscious mind off as he performs his pre-shot visualizations. After the shot, I help the golfer free his mind from the pressure of concentration by striking up a conversation about anything but golf. In this way I become a part of the golfer's mental switching mechanism—in fact, to a fair degree, I *am* the golfer's switching mechanism.

But what does the golfer do when he doesn't have a professional caddy on his bag? This is where anchoring comes in.

In its broadest application, anchoring is a technique formulated to change the mind from a losing mode to a winning or "peak experience" one. But, in addition, its particular application to golf is as the ignition key—the on-off switch—that takes us through the successive states of awareness, suppression and release of conscious thought.

Cutting the Ignition Key

As with creative visualization, the golfer has to be in a state of deep relaxation to begin the cutting of the brain's ignition key from the technique of anchoring. Visualization is central to developing an anchoring system, and the more practiced the golfer is at forming mental pictures the better the anchors work.

While an anchoring key is central to the on-off switching demands of competitive golf, anchoring keys can be cut for a myriad of other situations in life where an existing mental reflex or habit is in need of change. For example, the early-morning ringing of the alarm clock will trigger a negative reaction in most people, one that stays with them throughout the day as a mood of disgruntlement. But what if they were to respond positively to the alarm clock's ringing? What if they could change their brain's default reaction to the alarm clock from a negative to a positive one? How much more pleasant might a person's day become if the alarm clock triggered a positive response at the start of the day, rather than a negative one? Anchoring can bring this about.

Anchors can be developed to meet any specific need, and plucked from the mental toolbox at will. This is how the golfer creates anchors:

- He goes through his preferred relaxation exercise so that he feels relaxed, warm and peaceful. Then he breathes in through his nose for a count of eight, holds his breath for a count of 10, and breathes out through his mouth for a count of 12, working on this until he can do it without counting, and remembering to breathe in through his diaphragm from the bottom up.

- Now he turns on his mental television set—his imagination—and pictures himself, tense and negative from the target stimulus, be it the alarm clock or the domineering conscious thought that's trying to prevent his subconscious from delivering its best golf stroke. He sees himself frowning, complaining, unlucky, playing poorly—locked, that is, into a negative and losing mode. Once he's able to see clearly in his imagination what he looks and feels like in these circumstances, he makes his consciousness intrude with the determination that he doesn't want that look and feeling any more. Then he sees himself picking up a pot of paint and hurling it at the television screen of his imagination, totally obliterating the picture.

- He watches as the paint runs down the imaginary screen, dissolving the picture as it goes. He says to himself as the negative picture disintegrates, "I don't want that feeling any more. I don't need that feeling any more. There, it's gone."

- Now he goes back to his blank screen and visualizes himself in peak experience mode, 10 feet tall and bulletproof. If he's creating an anchor or switching system for use on the golf course, he sees himself being relaxed and confident, with an unshakably high expectation of success. He relives a time when he felt on top of the world, when he had that Midas touch, was playing like a wizard and could do no wrong. Alternatively, if he's trying to change his negative reaction to, say, the alarm clock going off, he pictures himself feeling marvelous in the morning at the prospect of another happy and fulfilling day. He remembers how he felt when he was like that, and pictures himself as others would have seen him in that cheery and positive frame of mind.

• When the memory and visualization have become crystal-clear (by this time he may find he's smiling to himself), he sets about creating a physical trigger that will conjure up those positive vibes in his subconscious any time he wants them. A simple way of doing this is by forming his fist into a particular grip, one that he wants to become unique and special to himself. It could be with his thumb jammed between his first two fingers, or his two middle fingers clenched while the index and little one poke out—anything, as long as he can remember it and repeat it at will. Then he does something with this specially gripped fist, like slapping his other arm, or beating his chest, or tapping his head. He could even develop a variation on Tiger Woods' triumphant trademark of punching the air when a vital putt drops. Whatever. The important elements are that he creates a physical signal or trigger that's personal and special to him, that can't be confused with any other gesture he habitually makes, and that is related specifically to either the circumstances that were previously creating the negative or otherwise unwanted default response, or to his on-course switching rhythm. He might add an audible element to the anchoring recipe, such as saying "Yeah!" out loud to himself, or "You're onto it!" or "You've got it!" The anchor or triggering mechanism has to be unique and consistent, and it mustn't be confused with anything but the specific behavior he is trying to modify or entrench.

• Now he wipes the entire picture off his imaginary television screen, and repeats the steps from 2 to 6 at least twice.

If he practices this technique twice a day for at least three weeks, his subconscious will begin to recognize the gesture of the special fist, the air-punching and the "Yeah!" as signals that are intended to switch it into a positive mode, or to switch off conscious thought so his subconscious is free to execute the golf stroke.

Whether it's the on-off switching of his conscious mind during a game of golf, or altering his responses to the alarm going off in the morning, his reactions will have been pre-programmed to produce a positive and constructive behavior.

In his mental toolbox of anchors he has a key to preferred behaviors that is as efficient and effective as the ignition key of a car.

Feel, and Where It Comes From

There are only 14 clubs in the golf bag, but between the drive and the putt there's an enormous range of distances and circumstances to which each one can be applied. Club selection is not determined by distance alone, though distance is usually the first consideration in choosing one. As a result, no one club is ever employed in precisely the same way every time. Each shot is unique.

Golf would be an easier game to play if it was possible to put exactly the same physical effort into each stroke. But to do that would require far more than the 14 clubs permitted. Instead, the golfer has to vary his physical input to some degree to suit the circumstances. The cornerstone of consistency though is to confine the variation of the physical effort to as narrow a range as possible.

In my experience, the world's best golfers hit the ball within a range of 70–80 percent of their physical capacity, with most shots played at about 75 percent effort. That gives a potential variation in effort of 5 percent either way with any given club. To extract the maximum distance from any club they may put up to 80 percent of their potential effort into the stroke. To get the ball to travel the minimum distance for any club, they reduce their physical input to as little as 70 percent of their capacity. If the effort required to reach the target area falls outside that variation of 5 percent either way, they chose another club.

The ability to vary the physical effort across that narrow range is what is known as "feel," and to me it's one of the most important factors in the game.

You've got to have the mechanics right, but golf is a game of feel. Anyone starting out in the game has to get the fundamentals right, but the key to improvement after that is developing feel. In golf every shot is different but you've got only 14 clubs, and it's the ability to vary the performance that you extract from the club that makes the difference between winning and losing.

I define feel as listening to your body, of being aware of how it's feeling on any given day, and knowing how that feeling will translate into a stroke within that narrow range of physical effort. The more subtle the variation you're able to introduce into the stroke, the greater your feel.

In a later chapter I'll reveal some tips on how to develop feel, but to illustrate the concept here is the comparison of two of the game's greats, Nick Faldo and Lee Trevino.

Faldo in his prime was one of the most mechanical players I've ever seen. He was extremely precise in his club selection and, as far as possible, he set out to play each stroke with exactly the same amount of power, exactly the same swing. Being mechanical, which is the opposite to having feel, has worked well for him, but mechanical players at that level of competition are very few and far between. As he's got older he's become less of a mechanical player and brought more feel into his game.

Before beginning the run of successes that brought him three British Opens and three Masters titles, Faldo was having trouble with his swing. At the age of 18 he had been the youngest ever winner of the English Amateur Championship but, by the early 1980s when he had been on the professional circuit for half a decade, he became convinced that his swing was badly flawed, limiting his potential. By 1985 he was so worried about it that he pulled out of Tony Jacklin's Ryder Cup team rather than risk his swing letting him down. Then, under the tutelage of English-born coach David Leadbetter, he set about methodically changing it. It took him two years to get it right but by sheer determination and endless practice he nailed it in the end.

It was that doggedness that put the sameness—though also the reliability—into his performance, and allowed him to make a virtue of a mechanical approach, which would be a limiting factor in almost any other player. He displayed it most dramatically in 1987 when he produced 18 consecutive pars to beat American Paul Azinger in the British Open at Muirfield.

Mechanical he may have been, but he was, and remains, one of the true greats.

Lee Trevino is the exact opposite, and he's fascinating to watch. He's a guy whose physical strength may not be as great as a lot of his peers, but the way he works his way around the course is amazing. Where Faldo plays one shot pretty much like any other, Trevino concocts something different and special for each one. Lee's the ultimate feel player. He's highly unorthodox.

From a poverty-stricken background, Texas-born Mexican-American Trevino got into golf because his home was next to a course. He joined the Marines at 17 and represented them in competitions in several eastern countries. By the time he was discharged in 1961, he was a hotshot, and he set about making money out of golf by hustling. One of his tricks for cranking up the stakes was to offer to play with only one club, a rusty old three iron. Another was to use a soft-drink bottle wrapped in adhesive tape as a club, and in pitch-and-putt competitions he'd take down wealthy opponents who were using conventional clubs. It was feats like these, combined with a swing that kept the club traveling down the line for longer than any other player, and a patter that drove some of his competitors to absolute distraction, that made the "Merry Mex" the godfather of feel.

Over the years I have traipsed many a course in Trevino's company, and I was there again on the day in 2001 when Tiger Woods had his only competitive encounter with the aging star. Tiger and Jack Nicklaus were playing Trevino and Sergio Garcia, and even though Trevino was 62 years old it was a match that Tiger had looked forward to.

Some of the shots Lee pulled off were extraordinary, and it was a lesson in subtlety to see how he attacked the course. Even today he's a genius of shot-making, the ultimate feel player.

The Tortures of Temperament

Talk of feel in the context of modern golf inevitably leads to a discussion of temperament. Lee Trevino might be the ultimate feel player, and Nick Faldo the ultimate mechanical one but, stylistically different as they are, no one could argue that either player lacks the temperament for top golf. However, the same could not be said for Tommy Bolt: his success in the game was achieved despite his unruly temperament rather than because of it.

Undoubtedly the ideal temperament for golf, in my opinion, is the unflappable serenity of Ernie "The Big Easy" Els. People that watch Els envy the way he seems immune to the frustrations and vexations that are at the heart of most golfers' love-hate affair with the game. The drive that skews off into a bunker, or the putt that lips the hole draw nothing from Els but a wry smile. His clubs don't need swimming lessons.

But that's just Ernie. He makes keeping the lid on his frustrations seem easy. It's a lot harder for most other people. And I think that bottling it all up may prove to be as counterproductive on the golf course as going berserk and breaking or throwing clubs. Els has much the same reaction to success as to disappointment. He gets no more excited at the putt that drops than at the one that lips the cup.

So is it possible to achieve a balance between the need to let off steam and the need to stay in control of your emotions?

I say there is, and it's up to the individual to find it. Temperament is part of the individual personality and it's very difficult to tell what the "right" temperament is. Everybody's different. For example, Tiger's temperament is quite volatile, and his way of dealing with the times he's angry at himself is to let it all out then and there—usually by whacking the bag with the club. At times like those, I keep clear of the bag. But with Tiger it's over and forgotten after that. It's out of his system and he doesn't let it affect his game from then on.

It's the same with his famous punching of the air when he pulls off a great shot. That's a case of letting out the tension too. Once it's done it's over and forgotten about, and he just continues with the next shot.

If you've got a volatile personality and you need to get the frustration out of you, provided you can get it all out then and there and go on to the next shot, you should do it. The worst thing you can do in golf is to let the anger build up, because then you're in the grip of tension. Golf is a game of feel, and if you let the tension build up in you, out goes your feel.

If you're going to show frustration at all, you've got to do it right there on the spot, and get it out of your system.

However, the balancing factor against releasing tension by outbursts of anger is the encouragement it can give your opponents. Because I was grounded in the hard, physical school of rugby, I understand only too well the need to play your cards close to your chest whatever your field of competition. In rugby, nothing puts smiles on the faces of the opposing players like someone losing his temper. Rugby is all about head-to-head physical clashes, and in that context emotional volatility is a weakness that opposing players will instantly pick up on and ruthlessly exploit. A short-tempered player will be relentlessly needled by the opposition in the hope that he'll crack, at which point he becomes a liability to his team's otherwise cohesive structure.

There's not the same necessity in golf to suppress your emotions—provided, of course, that you gather them back in before the next shot. But even so, emotional outbursts can be a signal to the opposition that you're wilting under the pressure, and no true competitor in any sport does anything that offers unnecessary encouragement to the opponent.

There are no hard and fast rules about how emotional—or emotionless—you should be in golf. You've got to balance the good that an emotional outburst can do you against the good it does your opponent.

Achieving that balance is critical to achieving the state of mind that produces the ultimate expression of individual sporting prowess: the peak experience.

12

The Paradox of the Peak Experience

Happiness is a long walk with a putter.

—Greg Norman

Despite the fact that we won it, the Buick Open in Flint, Michigan, was not the perfect lead-up to the 2002 PGA championship for Tiger and me. Tiger was certainly playing well, following his first-round 67 at Warwick Hills with his best round of the year to that point, a 63 on the par-72 course. He finished off with a 71 and a 70 to win by four shots, but for both of us it was a discomforting tournament. The Buick Open always attracts huge crowds, it was hot, and alcohol was being sold on the course. On the 17th hole on the final day, I came close to blows with a drunken spectator constantly heckling Tiger and his playing partner, Esteban Toledo.

So it was with a sense of relief that we escaped to the PGA Championship at the Hazeltine course in Chaska, Minnesota, the following week. Hazeltine isn't a regular PGA Tour venue, so the local crowd was especially appreciative of a field that included 102 of the world's top 105 players. In the final round Tiger was six strokes behind the eventual winner, Rich Beem, after bogeying the 13th and 14th, but then staged a phenomenal run of birdies on each of the last four holes to finish just one stroke back. Beem had to pull out a final-round 66, including an eagle at the 13th and a 35-foot birdie putt at the 16th, to hold him off.

But it was in this tournament—albeit on the previous morning when Tiger was finishing the rain-delayed second round—that he produced the finest golf shot I've seen. On the par-four 18th, with a 30 mph wind battering at him, Tiger found himself squeezed into a narrow fairway bunker 202 yards from the pin. The ball was just four yards from the lip of the bunker, and there was barely room for him to get in to address it. Once there he found himself peering through a wall of lofty pines directly between himself and the hole. Most other players would have grabbed the sand wedge and contented themselves with getting back onto the fairway with as clear a shot at the green as possible. They'd have accepted the sacrifice of a stroke rather than risk losing two or more in a tangle with the pines.

Not Tiger.

Instead he chose the three iron, and proceeded to slam the ball out of the bunker with enough loft on it to—barely—clear the trees. He constructed the shot so that the ball landed on the edge of the green and, to the delight and amazement of the gallery clustered round it, rolled to within 15 feet of the cup.

Tiger's playing partners that day were Ernie Els and David Toms, and they were so awestruck that they stood back and allowed Tiger to walk onto the green by himself while they joined the crowd in applause for a brilliantly devised and executed shot. Tiger then putted in for a birdie.

That three-iron bunker shot on Hazeltine's 18th took my breath away. It was even better than the previous best I'd seen: the 213-yard six iron Tiger hit from a fairway bunker, again to within 15 feet of the pin, to beat New Zealander Grant Waite by a single shot on the 18th at the Canadian Open the previous year.

The Hazeltine three iron was Tiger Woods at his very best. That shot was the embodiment of what every golfer—every sportsperson—is seeking to achieve: the peak experience.

That shot was golf played while Tiger was totally in the zone.

The most amazing thing about it was not that Tiger made it seem both achievable and effortless, but that he was in a state of palpable serenity when he hit it. He had responded to the challenge not by putting greater physical or mental effort into the shot, but by recognizing an opportunity where others would have seen a difficulty, and by devising a strategy within his skill range to suit the circumstances.

Fear of the consequences of muffing the shot never entered his head.

The "Try Harder" Fallacy

People everywhere, in all sports and individual endeavors, are forever being told that the harder they try the more successful they'll become. They're admonished: "If at first you don't succeed, try, try again." The corollary is that if you fail at something it's because you didn't try hard enough. But that sort of advice fails to recognize the true nature of failure which, like success, is simply another learning experience—an information-gathering exercise. It also fails to recognize that telling the subconscious to "try harder" only confuses it. People who tell you to "try harder" are confusing conscious desire with subconscious execution. Desire is, of course, the first prerequisite for achieving anything, but it's how a golfer manages and expresses that desire that decides whether or not they make it into the zone, whether or not they achieve the peak experience. Consciously trying harder, either to concentrate or to hit the ball with more power, won't get them there. In a game like golf, the harder you try the worse you do.

One of the hardest triers in the game, the club-flinging "Terrible" Tommy Bolt, used to describe golf as a game "where guts and blind devotion will net you absolutely nothing but an ulcer."

Isn't there a contradiction, a grand paradox, in a statement like that? Perhaps, but, the building of desire aside, trying to impose our conscious will on our subconscious mind is a recipe for failure. And that goes for all sport, not just golf. The principle behind all practice and training, physical and mental, is to remove the need to consciously try to perform well on the day. It's done by stocking the hard drive of the subconscious with all the data it's likely to need *before* it's called on to perform. Then once the golfer gets out there on the course, the concept of "trying" gives way to the concept of "applying."

Effect without conscious effort—that's the formula.

To put it another way, the prescription for success in sport is to "try to succeed by not consciously trying." The Zen masters of Japan call this paradox "effortless effort."

Setting goals, visualizing, writing affirmations and practicing awareness—and, of course, practicing physically on the course, the driving range and the putting green—comprise the "effort" part of "effortless effort." But having put in all this effort so far, the problem is that people tend to assume that the only way to express it in competition is by exercising tight mental control. After all, improvement in golf or anything else requires an investment of time and effort, and the bigger the investment the keener we are not to squander it.

Fair enough, but many people make the mistake of protecting their investment by trying to impose their conscious mind, their will, on the workings of the subconscious. They seem to think that the conscious mind is in some way superior to the subconscious, that when it comes to playing a golf stroke the conscious mind needs to be consciously instructing the subconscious how to go about it.

But that's just not the way it works.

The conscious and subconscious minds are not master and servant, but equal partners. Each has its own separate and distinct abilities which, if allowed to, mesh perfectly to produce perfect results.

The trick is to separate their functions, to prevent their functions from overlapping.

The thing about the subconscious is that it's just a machine, just a computer: it'll obey instructions to the letter, even if those instructions stop it from doing the very job the conscious mind really wants it to do. Tommy Bolt's "guts and determination" are functions of the conscious mind, along with mental and physical training. Hitting a golf ball in the heat of competition to a predetermined direction, distance and trajectory are functions of the subconscious. If the two separate functions overlap, the result is a bad golf shot.

Once this essential contradiction, this paradox, is fully understood, the golfer is on his way to expressing his true and full potential. He's on his way to the peak experience.

Ten Feet What?

What exactly is this sensation they call the peak experience, this being in the zone? Most sportspeople experience it at some time in their careers. It's that magical sensation when you feel as though you can do anything, you're 10 feet tall and bulletproof.

You're unbeatable.

You're sublime.

Achieving the peak experience, which is another term for expressing your full and true potential, is the aim of all mental and physical training, regardless of the sport. Yet for most sportspeople the peak experience occurs entirely unexpectedly, for no apparent reason. Most people can't figure out what precipitated their passage into the zone, or why, and they're left with a dazed sense of wonder at the way they played, at the confidence they felt.

You see it in the purple patches many golfers find themselves going through in the course of a round. For two or three holes they feel in complete control of the ball, the club, the swing, and they seem to be able to do no wrong.

Then, of course, the sensation passes and they're back to whacking it into the trees and water hazards just as they did before. It can be years before that happy coincidence of factors returns to produce that sensation in them again.

But it needn't be that way. Ultimately they should be able to step into peak experience mode on the first tee, and sustain it to the 18th. Tiger Woods was in the zone when he hit that miracle shot on Hazeltine's 18th that Saturday morning. And he was back in it the following day when he pulled off four birdies in the last four holes to all but snatch the 2002 PGA title from Rich Beem.

Nor was his performance at Hazeltine an accident. Throughout the glorious 2001 and 2002 seasons he slipped into the zone as easily as he had slipped into the Masters green jacket for the first time in 1997. He had his father Earl to thank for laying the groundwork during his childhood for the repeated peak experiences he enjoyed later, but it was Tiger himself who built on that foundation, using the same principles described in this book.

The phenomenon of the peak experience occurs in all sports, and psychologists have isolated eight components to it. They are:

MENTAL QUIET

Mental quiet is often the aspect of the peak experience that sportspeople remember most fondly. They're overwhelmed by a sense of inner peace and tranquillity, no matter how important the game might be, nor how much pressure their opponents are exerting. Time seems to have slowed down, allowing for total and effortless concentration. They cease to be aware of distractions—such as the noise or the silence of spectators, or of any stimuli irrelevant to the task in hand.

PHYSICAL RELAXATION

Sportspeople in the zone are free of physical tension. Their muscles relax and take on heightened tonal and sensory qualities, especially during periods of the most intense activity—that is, during the execution of the golf stroke itself.

IN THE NOW

Once in the zone, the mind and the body seem to discover a perfect unison in which there is no past and no future—only "the now." Execution of shots is automatic and effortless, and occurs without conscious thought. Whatever happened before or may happen later, good or bad, is unimportant, inconsequential. All the energy is focused on this game, this shot, this moment.

CONFIDENCE AND OPTIMISM

Confidence and self-belief abound, whatever the match situation, during the peak experience. The golfer looks forward to the opposition playing well, because it gives him the opportunity to show he can play even better. Difficulties and challenges become opportunities. Errors become sources of vital information that ensure the success of the next stroke.

ENERGY

There is a feeling of extraordinary wellbeing in the zone. The player feels fit, happy, and in full control of events. He has boundless energy and seems incapable of weariness, mental or physical. He loves life. He smells the flowers.

AWARENESS

There is a sense of being fully attuned to the environment, of being able to soak up a boundless supply of information and influences helpful to his game, during a peak experience. The information is uniformly accurate, and the subconscious effortlessly selects the most useful and relevant data from among the deluge of messages being delivered by the highly tuned senses.

CONTROL

During a peak experience, knowledge seems to arrive, with a minimum of conscious thought, of what to do in any given situation, and how to do it. Results turn out to be exactly what was intended and expected. This results in an all-encompassing feeling of being in control of the situation. No matter what obstacles the course or the opponents throw up, the golfer in the zone knows how to deal with them.

IN A COCOON

All these characteristics are accompanied by a feeling of perfect safety, as if the player were protected by a notional barrier that excludes worry, doubt and fear—as if he was in a time warp or cocoon. Negative thoughts don't enter his mind. He is able to concentrate fully, his awareness insulated against extraneous data, his conscious mind and his subconscious working in perfect harmony.

Anyone who's had these eight sensations at the same time has had a peak experience, has been in the zone. Probably the nearest thing to it in any other facet of life is the experience of falling in love: it's an intensely personal and individual feeling, but unmistakable once it's hit. If anyone has to ask what it's like, it hasn't happened to them yet.

The Power of Expectation

We've seen that peak experiences can occur by accident, and that conscious thought is a barrier to their occurring, but if they're such a wonderful thing, what can we do to bring them about more often?

The answer, in a word, is "expectation."

The frequency with which the peak experience occurs is dependent on the player's level of expectation of success: the higher the expectation of success, the greater the frequency of peak experiences. Heightened expectation is a side effect of the techniques already described—the goal-setting, the visualization and the affirmations, while the anchors described in the previous chapter provide the triggers that can set off a peak experience.

But there's another factor involved. The length of a peak experience—the time the player remains in the zone—and the likelihood of it recurring are dependent on how he deals with it both while under its influence, and immediately afterwards.

The most important rule in dealing with a peak experience at these stages is not to question its validity. To react to a peak experience by consciously wondering if it's really happening is a certain means of breaking the spell. Such wondering encourages the consciousness to intrude, which has the effect of switching off the peak experience. Questioning the validity of the experience undermines the very basis on which it occurs, which is the accumulation of self-belief and heightened expectation produced by the mental exercises and training that created it in the first place.

The peak experience should be accepted as a right, as the logical outcome of the work that went into producing it, not as a freak occurrence beggaring belief.

Likewise, after it's happened the golfer should continue to accept its occurrence as a normal and desired state of mind, and not inadvertently drown the memory of it in negative affirmations back in the clubhouse. The golfer coming off the peak experience shouldn't allow himself to be amazed by what's happened. He shouldn't blurt out to all and sundry at the 19th, "I don't believe how well I played," or "I was incredibly lucky." To do so would be to inform his subconscious that the peak experience was a freak event, a sort of unreality or surreality that is, or should be, outside the scope of "normal" behavior.

The subconscious, which cannot distinguish between positive and negative outcomes, has no choice but to absorb as fact the interpretative spin that the conscious mind puts on any event. If the conscious mind tells the subconscious that the peak experience was a freak or unreal event, the subconscious will accept that interpretation without question, and set about guarding against it happening again.

Instead, the player who's enjoyed a peak experience should look upon it as the norm, the standard by which all future performances are measured—at least until the next peak experience raises the bar even further.

The peak experience is simply the normal outcome of an abnormal expectation of success. It's the expectation that's abnormal, not the experience. The simple equation is: raise the expectation of success, and the quality of the "normal" game rises to match the quality attained during the peak experience.

Entrenching this expectation in the subconscious removes fear and negativity from the nervous system, allowing performance to equal potential. To repeat the peak experience, the player has to cultivate an ever-rising expectation of success.

And how does the player raise his expectation of success? Firstly by not denigrating the peak experience either while it's happening, or when he's back in the clubhouse, and thereafter by continuing with goal-setting, affirmations and visualization to further trick the subconscious into accepting the peak experience as the new measure of what is normal.

In short, to raise the performance, crank up the expectations.

The Expectation Index

The relationship between expectation and performance is so important that it's worth taking a little time here to express it graphically.

At any stage in a golfer's career, he has imprinted on his subconscious a fair idea of where he ranks among other players. The handicap system sees to that. But as an exercise in the dynamics of expectation, the golfer might try converting his ranking to an index number, where a world-beater like Tiger Woods is on +10, and the incorrigible weekend whacker is on -10. The average or median player would thus be 0 on the scale. Though a player like Tiger Woods might be on +10, he's always trying and expecting to improve. To accommodate that potential for improvement, we need to set the top of the expectation range higher — at, say, +15.

Over the period of a single season, we could reasonably expect a player ranked, say, +1 to improve through experience and practice to perhaps +2. His level of performance will vary during the season but his improvement index would describe a growth-line from +1 to +2. This is expressed as the straight dotted line plotted on the following graph, where the player is labeled "Average."

Such an improvement pattern would be typical of a player who ranks himself on the basis of his performance—that is, on what he's done in the past—as distinct from ranking himself on his expectations of his true and full potential. This is a player who still believes it's "how you play on the day" that determines success, and he'll wait and see what happens on that day before he decides what level of success to expect thereafter.

Because he believes his ranking is a factor of his performance rather than his expectations, this player is vulnerable to both form slumps and purple patches. He improves naturally enough through practice and experience. He has his ups and downs, as plotted by the wiggly black line, and may even have a peak experience at some stage. But because he moulds his expectations to his performance, he inevitably follows his index line of modest improvement from +1 to +2 over the season. Even if he produces the occasional shocker of a game, his attitude of "it's how you play on the day" will probably ensure he's resilient enough to recover to meet his expectation index line.

EXPECTATION AND PERFORMANCE GRAPH

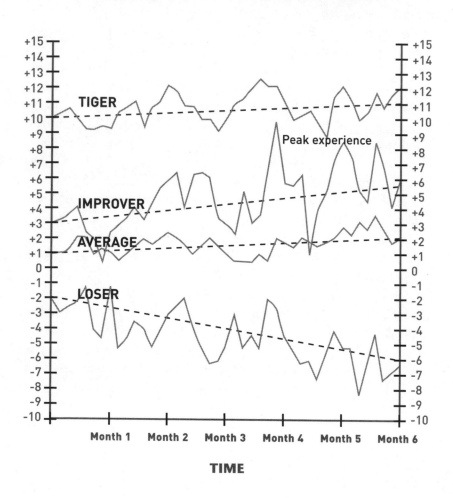

TIGER

Peak experience

IMPROVER

AVERAGE

LOSER

TIME

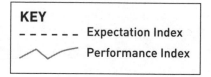

KEY
- - - - - Expectation Index
  Performance Index

Now let's look at the golfer who starts out on a performance and index ranking of, say, -2, at a time when he's already running into problems with, say, his swing. On the graph we've labeled this player "Loser" and, like Average, he too ranks himself on the basis of his past performances rather than his future ones. He knows that unless he addresses the problems with his swing, his performance will go into decline. His expectation index accordingly drops during the course of the season to, say, -6. His performance index will inevitably follow suit.

Now let's take the cheerier example of the golfer who understands the true relationship between expectation and performance. We'll call him "Improver." His goal-setting, visualization and affirmation exercises will have given him a pretty accurate idea of the level of improvement he can reasonably expect over the course of the season if he plays to his true and full potential—and it'll be a lot more ambitious than Average's rise from +1 to +2. If he starts with a performance index of, say, +3, he might reasonably expect to have improved to, say, +6 by the end of the season. That's three times the rate of improvement of Average, who based his expectations on his performance rather than the other way round. Such a level of improvement is possible for Improver because he realizes that his use of goal-setting, affirmations and visualization inevitably raises the expectation level in his subconscious, and his performance cannot help but rise to meet those expectations.

But isn't there the danger that Improver will set entirely unrealistic expectations of improvement, and then not be able to meet them? Sure, he could, especially at the start. But because mental training of the sort described in this book has its basis in honest self-awareness, he'll quickly adjust to any overshooting of his expectation level. He is, after all, charting his improvement daily on his master plan and in his weekly diary, and he'll very quickly come to distinguish between what is realistically attainable and what is plain fanciful.

To round out our analysis of the relationship between expectation and performance, we've given Tiger Woods top spot on the graph. We've already decided that he's at +10 on the performance graph, and we know that, while he can always improve, the increments will become smaller the better he gets. That's in the nature of improvement: the further you've gone, the less you've got to go. Accordingly, his expectation index might rise from +10 to only +11—the same modest increment as

Average. But in Tiger's case the difference expresses itself in whether he scores five victories on the PGA Tour or seven or nine.

Whoever the player, whatever the level of competition, performance is ultimately determined by informed expectation. Expect success, however you measure it, and it must arrive. And that grand feeling of the peak experience is the package it arrives in.

13

Harnessing Fear, Managing Pain

Laughter is the only way to react to some of the things that happen in golf, because if you didn't laugh you'd cry.

—Jack Nicklaus

Considering it's a non-contact sport with a relatively low physical input, golf exacts quite a toll on the bodies of players. Among the professionals, injury is a constant threat, and unless they can sort the damage out by rest or exercise, they often have to resort to surgery. Of my three long-term employers, only Raymond Floyd managed to get by without going under the knife for golf-related injuries. Tiger Woods had to have surgery on his knee at the end of the 2002 season, and Greg Norman had arthroscopic hip surgery in 2000 and shoulder socket surgery in 1998.

The four main injury sites in golfers are the lower back, the elbows, the hands/wrists and the shoulders, though the distribution of such injuries varies between amateurs and professionals. It also varies to a certain extent between men and women.

Of injuries to amateurs, most are to the lower back (35 percent) and elbows (33 percent), while hands and wrists account for 20 percent and shoulders for 12 percent. Women generally suffer more injuries to their elbows than to their lower backs. Among the professionals it's the hands and wrists that are most at risk—especially among women, who suffer more than half their injuries in those areas—followed by the lower back, shoulders and elbows.

Generally speaking, the professionals' injuries are overwhelmingly (80 percent) due to overuse, whereas among amateurs that is, people averaging two rounds a week—only 25 percent of injuries develop this way. A further 21 percent of amateur injuries come from "fat" shots (hitting the ground with the club) and 19 percent from poor swing mechanics. Over-swinging (swinging too hard or fast), twisting the trunk during the swing, failure to warm up properly, and changing their grip or swing account for most other amateur injuries.

Interestingly, it's the lower handicap (0–9) players among the amateurs who are more likely to be injured (67 percent), compared to those on 18+ handicaps (59 percent). As you'd expect, golfers over 50 years of age tend to have more injuries than younger ones, but the difference between the two groups isn't that great: 65 percent for those over fifty compared to 58 percent for those under.

And those are just the physical injuries. Most of the world's 70 million golfers would concede the game generates vastly more emotional than physical pain. It seems pain, physical and emotional, is an unavoidable by-product of golf, as of life.

But it's never stopped people playing the game, and it never will.

Everything we do in life is risky: the mere fact of living is life-threatening. Accordingly fear and pain are as much a part of golf as they are of any facet of life. These statistics notwithstanding, the greatest physical danger the golfer encounters is in getting to the course: more damage is done to golfers by motor accidents on the way to playing a round than by actually playing. Once on the course, probably the biggest physical danger is of getting hit by an errant golf ball, something that's happened a couple of times to me. In 1978, for example, I was knocked out cold and carted off to hospital to get six stitches in my head after being hit by a wayward shot on the 18th while caddying for American Loren Roberts in the Australian Open pro-am. But such things are freak occurrences, and no reasonable person would be scared off golf by the fear of the physical pain that might result from playing it.

So physical fear can largely be discounted as a consideration in playing golf. However, physical fear isn't the only kind. Of real significance to everyone's game of golf is that other kind of fear: fear of failure.

Fear

At some point in their career, every golfer encounters, and has to come to terms with, fear of failure. It's a constantly recurring emotion and, as such, is the golfer's most powerful emotional ally. Yes, ally. Fear is a good thing. Fear is your friend.

If you lack fear—and some people do—then you are seriously, perhaps life-threateningly, flawed. Or you simply haven't built up a strong enough desire to win, to succeed.

Fear derives from the strongest and most basic urge of all life forms: the desire to live. (The second strongest is the sex drive, the urge to perpetuate oneself by producing children). Thus, fear is the barometer of threat to life, and those who don't experience it aren't really living.

Few golfers ever lose their fear of failure—nor would they want to. Those queasy pre-game feelings in the pit of the stomach are pure fear of failure, and some golfers get just about tied up in knots by them before a big game.

But pre-game attacks of the butterflies should be treasured by the golfer, because they are the measure of his desire to win. Uncomfortable as they may be, they are a vital resource that, once harnessed, give the golfer's game a winning edge.

The trick to harnessing them is first to welcome them, to own them. The golfer should let them fester away inside him during the pre-game preparation, knowing that this is just the conscious mind explaining to the subconscious the importance of succeeding in the challenge they are about to embark upon. The trick is not to suppress or fight the nauseous butterfly feelings, but to package them into a conscious message to the subconscious.

Harnessing the innate power of the fear of failure begins during the pre-game warm-up period, which extends from the time the golfer gets out of the car in the golf-club parking lot to when he's walking to the first tee. In between stretching exercises and visits to the driving range and practice green, the golfer mentally rehearses all the skills he will be called on to perform in the course of the round. This involves repeating the visualizations and affirmations he's built into his daily mental training routine, and reminding himself of where this particular match fits among the intermediate and long-term goals on his master plan, and the short-term goals in his weekly diary. What he's doing by such revision is refreshing his subconscious memory of the particular skill files it's about to have to draw upon. He's telling his subconscious, "Have these particular skill files to hand, because we're shortly going to need them."

Throughout this time the golfer is consciously welcoming and tak-ing ownership of his fear of failure symptoms, his butterflies. He can do this most effectively by breathing exercises. They will not only have the effect of calming the nausea in his stomach, but more importantly will relax both his body and mind. He will thereby ensure that his subcon-scious is in the best state to receive and absorb the messages that will shortly start flowing in as he exercises his awareness of all the factors that will influence his strokes. He'll be conscious of the way that relax-ation slows down the pattern of his brain-waves, and that the slower they become the more receptive his subconscious will be to the messages it receives.

The golfer's final exercise in dealing with his pre-game fear of fail-ure is a visualization, in which he sees himself switching off his con-scious mind and, at the same time, switching the butterflies off too. This works remarkably effectively if it's connected to his regular conscious-ness switching-off (anchoring) procedures, the ones he employs to turn responsibility for the execution of the first shot of the day over to his subconscious. He sees and feels in advance all his fears melting away at that instant when he cuts his conscious mind out of the shot-execution loop. He sees and feels himself switching his conscious mind on and off thereafter as he moves from one shot to the next.

Like physical fear, fear of failure is a great servant, but a destruc-tive master, so the golfer needs to be in control of it, not at its mercy.

It's helpful to remember that anyone in any sport or facet of life has to feel fear to know courage, and that the courageous person is not the one who knows no fear, but the one who recognizes and harnesses his fear and makes it work for him.

Reining in the Waggles

Fear of failure has found a unique way to express itself on the golf course, other than by way of the pre-game butterflies. It's "the waggles," which used to be a common component of many players' pre-shot rou-tines, but in the last few decades has fallen into disuse somewhat, in part because it gave rise to an essentially psychological problem for some players who adopted it.

An old Scottish golfing adage was, "As ye waggle, so shall ye swing." Even as recently as the late 1960s one of golf's greatest teachers, "The Silver Scot" Tommy Armour (U.S. Open champion 1927, PGA 1930, British Open 1931), recommended waggling the hips as a last action before launching into the backswing. Its value was not only in getting the backswing motion started smoothly, but also in predetermining the pace and power of the total stroke. A player with, say, a fast and jerky swing, could slow it down and steady it—by slowly and steadily waggling his hips a couple of times beforehand.

The downside of this practice was that, once started, some nervous or indecisive golfers couldn't stop waggling: instead of launching into their backswing, they just stood their waggling their hips.

A similar difficulty arose with putts, where again the problem was essentially that of continuing the pre-shot routine without ever getting round to making the putt itself. The putting problem is sometimes referred to as "the yips," and even some great golfers have fallen victim to it. Germany's Bernhard Langer (Masters champion 1985), for whom I occasionally caddied, went through three separate stages of his otherwise brilliant career when the putting yips all but destroyed his game. Each time, though, he found a way of overcoming them.

What probably happens is that when someone is standing over the ball and continually waggling their hips—or even the club—their minds won't focus on what they're trying to do, to the degree that they can't draw back the clubhead. They're probably saying to themselves, "I've got to keep my head still" or "I've got to do this or that," and their minds can't absorb it all.

In short, they've failed to switch off their conscious mind and let the subconscious take over the execution of the shot. Indecision in such situations is caused by the conscious and subconscious minds being in conflict, with the subconscious being bombarded with conscious thoughts at odds with the information it's gathered from its hard disk files. At best the outcome is a lousy stroke or putt. At worst it's no stroke or putt at all.

The way to stop it may involve just eliminating the hip-waggle itself, though this may be too radical a response for those for whom it's an entrenched part of their pre-shot routine.

Alternatively—or additionally—the answer lies in a combination of the final pre-shot visualization, and in the consciousness switching-off mechanism. It's the old principle of visualizing the shot backwards, with the last visualization before the backswing being of the instant in which the clubhead makes contact with the ball. This visualization is easy, because the clubhead is right there in front of you, just a fraction behind the ball. What the golfer sees and what he visualizes at that point are therefore pretty much one and the same thing. All the golfer has to do is keep the clubhead completely still, and as close to the contact point on the back of the ball as possible.

Then he applies the switching mechanism: he simply disconnects his conscious mind from this point and lets the subconscious take over to execute the shot. In this the golfer will be hugely helped by the anchoring techniques described earlier. The physical anchoring trigger might be to tap one finger on the club's shaft at the same time as he employs an audible trigger, such as mumbling to himself, "Yes, I'm switched off." Firing the trigger releases the backswing.

With practice and persistence, both "the waggles" and "the yips" can be eliminated in this way.

Pain

In dealing with the pain to be encountered on the golf course, it's difficult to draw distinctions between the physical and the emotional. Science doesn't yet know where or how—or even if—the human brain distinguishes between the physical pain that arises from injury or exertion, and the emotional pain that is the result of losing, of failure. All pain feels pretty much the same to the conscious mind and, if the subconscious can tell the difference, it hasn't yet given up the secrets of how it does it.

Pain is as much a part of life and golf as is pleasure, and its very existence implies that endurance in the face of it is an essential life-skill. The trick is to make pain endurable, and the first step towards that is understanding, as far as possible, the way it works—its mechanisms. This will help the golfer to own his pain, just as he must learn to own his fear, because he can't manage something he's in denial of.

Western medicine breaks pain down into two varieties, acute and chronic. In the sporting context, acute pain is that precipitated by damage to the mind or body, and it goes away as and when the person recovers. Chronic pain is the sort that sticks around, as if it's got a life of its own, either after the damage has been made good and/or when all apparent traces of it have disappeared.

Nerve endings, found in nearly every tissue of the body, are the sense organs that first pick up pain signals from, say, a wrist injured in a "fat" shot. The signals, the data, are transmitted along the nerve cells (also called fibers) to a region in the spinal cord called the dorsal horn. This is a collection of nerve cells that passes the information on to tracts that travel on up the spinal cord and mostly end in a part of the brain called the thalamus. From there they're distributed to their various other destinations in the brain, including the cerebral cortex, the brain's outer layer that contains our consciousness. Cortical receiving areas seem to be where the pain signals and some of their emotional baggage get sorted into perceptions (though perception can also occur without the cortex being involved).

Other types of pain signals, such as those for intestinal colic, travel along similar pathways, taking time out to trigger nausea and, in the worst cases, vomiting reflexes on the way. These are the mechanics of the nervous sensation we call the butterflies.

A peculiar thing about the pathway that pain travels along is that it's a two-way street: not only do pain signals pass from the damaged area to the brain, but pain-inhibiting signals also travel in the opposite direction—from the brain towards the damaged area. Somewhere within the central nervous system the opposing signals meet and, to vastly varying degrees, more or less cancel each other out.

Medical science is unsure exactly where it is along the nerve pathways that the pain signals and the painkiller signals actually meet. What they do know is that a range of external chemical painkillers—analgesics can be administered to inhibit the transmission and perception of pain in the central nervous system. The best known of these analgesics is morphine, which acts locally at the site of the injury, more generally in the dorsal horn area of the spinal cord, and within the brain itself. It can deaden mental pain no less than the physical variety, which is why it's such an addictive substance.

The way analgesics like morphine work in the dorsal horn led scientists to formulate the gateway control theory of pain. The basic principle of this theory is that the use of analgesics like morphine "closes the gate" on the incoming pain signals, thereby preventing most or all of the pain from registering in the brain. Within the brain and spinal cord, natural chemicals called "opioid peptides" are produced which, because they work in a similar way to morphine, are often referred to as "the body's own morphine."

All of which raises the question of whether we can control pain by generating these opioid peptides at will. To which the short answer is yes—at least to some degree.

There is plenty of anecdotal evidence of pain control by auto-suggestion, which is the technique of the conscious mind telling the subconscious that the pain doesn't really exist, in the expectation that the subconscious will believe this message and trigger the brain's pain-suppressing devices. It works, though the degree to which it does so varies hugely from one individual to the next.

The only surefire means of on-demand pain relief are analgesics—everything, that is, from aspirin and morphine to general anaesthetic—as well as acupuncture, surgery and physical therapy.

That said, there are psychological methods of pain management—endorsed, if not yet fully understood, by medical science—which complement the standard "RICE" formula for immediate treatment of physical injuries. RICE stands for Resting the injured area for 24–48 hours; applying Ice to it for five to 20 minutes every hour until the heat is gone from it; Compressing the area with elastic bandages for 30 minutes at a time with a 15-minute spell in between; and Elevating the injured area to help reduce swelling.

Relieving Pain

The two most widely accepted psychological techniques of pain relief that can be applied without professional assistance are relaxation and imagery—and inevitably the two are closely linked.

Given that stress and tension increase the amount of pain we feel, it stands to reason that the techniques we covered in the chapter on relaxation will, on their own, reduce the perception of pain, be it physical or mental. They're especially useful in managing the pain immediately after a physical injury. On a longer timescale the imagery technique described below can be incorporated into the ongoing pain-management system as well.

As soon as possible after the injury, physical or mental, has occurred, the player should focus on relaxing his whole body by employing the breathing techniques described earlier. Tension—muscular or mental—heightens the perception of pain, so bringing himself into as relaxed a state as soon as possible is the first step in managing pain. Once the pain has settled into its medium-term recovery levels, it's time to employ the other psychological pain-management technique, imagery.

This is pure visualization, and it goes right to core of the relationship between the conscious and the subconscious mind, and the principles on which this book is based. Essentially it's a case of the player using his imagination to transport himself away from his pain-filled environment to a painless one. Like all the techniques described in this book, the more imagery is practiced, the more effective it'll be. It's a technique that can eventually be employed anywhere, anytime.

Here's how the hurt golfer goes about it.

He starts out in a comfy chair or on a bed with the lights dimmed, and with no danger of interruption. Having gotten as comfortable as possible, he regulates his breathing so that it's steady and full. He slowly fills his lungs with as much air as he can take in, then just as slowly releases it. He repeats this about a dozen times, or until his breathing pattern has slowed right down into a comfortable but minimal activity.

Now he starts to imagine himself in his favorite scene of peace and tranquillity. It may be at the beach with fluffy clouds floating overhead and the warm sun caressing him, and with little waves rustling along the shore.

Next he gradually introduces a sensation, such as warmth or coolness, to the area that the pain emanates from, be it the brain or the site of a physical injury. He feels the pleasant sensation slowly beginning to swamp the pain, overpowering it, replacing it. He imagines the pain being squeezed out, as though it were a liquid, by these ever-expanding pleasant sensations. Then he concentrates on enjoying, luxuriating in them.

Or He Could . . .

An alternative technique, once he's settled his breathing, would be to imagine his pain as a knife stuck in the area that's hurting—a knife that he's gradually pulling out. He feels the knife taking the pain with it as he withdraws it, and he revels in its absence once it's gone.

Again it's important to remember that auto-suggestion of all kinds is a skill. Nobody's born with it. It has to be developed. The better the person becomes at it, the more effective it will be in helping him manage his pain. Practiced in the context of the mental training techniques described in the book, it can become a remarkably effective method of pain relief.

Which is just as well, because there's a type of golfer who builds his game around inflicting mental pain on anyone unfortunate or unwise enough to fall for his tricks and wiles. This type of golfer is the gamer, the kind who employs the dark arts of gamesmanship to upset his competitors. In the next chapter we meet the gamer and learn how to respond to him by inflicting a particular pain in reprisal—the pain of frustration.

14

Gamesmanship

I play with friends, but we don't play friendly games.

—Ben Hogan

Seve Ballesteros used to say that he'd look into his opponents' eyes, shake their hands, pat their backs and wish them luck. But all the time he was thinking, "I'm going to bury you." That's the nature of competitiveness. It's the point at which the focus expands from the individual's play to include the opponent's. It's that point of realization, as the golfer approaches tee-off, that he's no longer alone, no longer operating in a vacuum occupied solely by himself. Now he faces the reality that the other people on the tee all want to beat him.

However, golfers can, if they so choose, go through an entire career without ever changing their focus from improving their own performance to lowering the performance of their opposition. They can continue to operate alone in the vacuum of their own abilities, oblivious to the opposition's tactics. And that's fine, but golf is really two games.

The first is played against oneself, the second against one's opponent. This book has so far only looked at the first of those games. Playing against yourself involves organizing all your resources, mental and physical, to work in harmony with each other. The other game involves creating disharmony in the minds of the opponent. It's called gamesmanship, and involves getting the opposition to beat themselves before they can get around to beating you. Tiger Woods refers to it as "the game within the game."

Gamesmanship is psychological warfare, and it's a legitimate competitive device with potentially devastating effects, though not always or necessarily for the intended target. Gamesmanship is an integral part of golf at any level, and it can make the difference between two players of equal ability. Also, it can provide the edge that distinguishes the habitual winner from the habitual also-ran.

No top player can survive in the game without at least an understanding of the principles of gamesmanship, and of how to recognize and combat them when the opposition resorts to them. By the same token, gamesmanship is not an indispensable weapon in the armory of the successful golfer, and not just because it's fairly easy to create defenses against it. The downsides of gamesmanship are that it's potentially self-deluding, and it's at least as likely to have a negative impact on the gamer as it is on the intended victim.

Gamesmanship works only if the target falls for it—and if the target doesn't fall for it, the gamer then has to deal with the psychological impact of being deprived of a weapon. A competitor with a habitual reliance on gamesmanship is thus vulnerable to an opponent who sees through the device and declines to be affected by it.

Gamesmanship is the art of negative suggestion, and relies on the opponent taking the suggestion aboard and performing to its implicitly lowered expectations. It works by disrupting the relationship between the opponent's conscious mind and his subconscious. The basic principle is to suggest to the opponent that circumstances are stacked against him, and then to rely on the opponent's conscious mind to pass this perception on to his subconscious, which performs accordingly—that is, short of his true and full potential. The more the opponent takes aboard the negative suggestions fed to him by the gamer, the worse he plays.

Take, for example, the old trick of bursting into a coughing fit just as the target is commencing his backswing. At this point the target has presumably switched off his conscious thought and turned the execution of the shot over to his subconscious. The effect of the coughing fit is to reactivate the conscious mind at precisely the moment it should be dormant. The conscious mind transmits the useless but audible data to the subconscious which, obediently but hopelessly, tries to incorporate it into the rest of the information it's processing into the stroke. The result? A botched shot.

Score one for the gamer.

This sort of ploy can also have a residual effect: the next time the target commences his backswing, his conscious mind will retain a nagging fear that the distraction will be repeated and, even if it isn't, the operation of his subconscious will be affected by the possibility that it might be.

Tiger Woods' father Earl understood this process precisely, and from early on in his son's golfing career he set about making him immune to it. His method began with Tiger agreeing not to talk at all during a round in which Earl pulled all the gamer's tricks he could think of, from dropping the golf bag in the middle of his backswing, to walking across his line of sight while he was lining up a putt. In case it got too much for Tiger, they had a code word that he could resort to. If Tiger used the code word, Earl quit the harassment. Tiger never used the code word, never spoke during these mind-toughening exercises—though he later reckoned that if looks could have killed, Earl wouldn't have survived his son's formative years.

The exercises worked. Tiger grew up virtually immune to the gamers he met and played on his rise to greatness. And these days if any spectators try to pick up where the opposition leaves off, he has me with my rugby player's glare and rottweiler's bark to remind them of their manners.

The Language of Gamesmanship

The main medium for communicating negative suggestions to opponents is language, both body and verbal. An acknowledged master of both in golf is the "Merry Mex," Lee Trevino, whose constant chatter, to opponents and spectators alike, could be devastatingly upsetting to his opponents. When he went to defend his British Open title at Muirfield in 1972, one of the English competitors, Neil Coles, confessed he couldn't concentrate with Trevino around, and asked the Royal and Ancient officials to let him play with somebody—anybody—else. Another time, when English great Tony Jacklin asked him if they could play in silence, Trevino replied, "Sure. You don't have to say a word." But then he added mischievously, "You just have to listen."

The best gamers in golf bring a wonderful extra element to the game, whether or not their gamesmanship works. Trevino attracted his own loyal gallery of spectators keen to see what tricks he could conjure up next, and how the intended victim would respond to them.

A standard weapon of the gamer is commiseration—sympathizing with the opponent over the difficult situation he's been placed in by the gamer. This introduces the opponent's consciousness to the idea that he's battling against some element other than merely the skill of the gamer. The other element may be bad luck, bad weather, a bad surface—whatever. The message is that the gamer is somehow immune to these negative effects and that the opponent is vulnerable to them. The gamer becomes solicitous: of course, he'd love to help the victim overcome the difficulties they both share, but really all he can do is feel sorry for the poor sucker.

A second common device is gratitude: the gamer in essence thanks his victim for making things easier for him, as if that was the victim's intention.

A third is the barefaced lie: the gamer says of his victim's fine tee shot, "Pity about that," as though its very excellence created more problems for the victim than the gamer.

The variations on such themes are infinite.

Developing the skills of gamesmanship takes time, though some people seem born to it. Lee Trevino developed them while representing the Marines in inter-services tournaments, and refined them afterwards as a means of finally escaping the poverty-stricken background in which he was raised. His antics with his rusty old three iron and his taped-up soft-drink bottles all helped raise the financial stakes in a game, while his chatter and skylarking reduced the likelihood of having to pay out at the end of the day. His childhood poverty, he was fond of remarking, provided his greatest incentive to make money out of golf, and his gamesmanship was a key element in his escaping the poverty trap.

The Actor in Every Gamer

Gamesmanship is essentially acting, and the most convincing actors are those who live the part they're playing. This requires the ability to live not only in the now, but also "in the then" or "in the maybe." As an exercise, it's essentially schizophrenic, and therefore as potentially dangerous to the gamer as to the target. Some people are cut out for it, some can cut themselves out for it, and some will never be any good at it no matter how hard they try.

The individual golfer doesn't have to learn to be a gamer, but he must of necessity develop defenses against gamesmanship, the single most effective of which is simply being aware of what the gamer's up to. The only way for the golfer to find out if gamesmanship offers any potential for improving his success rate is to try it out. He can start by quietly ingratiating himself with his intended victim, the aim being to trick the target's subconscious into being more amenable to the gamer's suggestions than to the target's.

Verbal suggestions can be backed up with supportive body language. The gamer's stifled giggle in response to a good shot may make the victim question his own values. The sad shake of the head when the target goes three-up with five to play may suggest the gamer hasn't been taking the match seriously up till now—but he's about to, so look out. And if the gamer goes three-up with five to play, a casual yawn might suggest he's got this far so effortlessly that the victim has long since squandered any chance of bridging the gap.

If, however, the individual golfer lacks the stomach for such enlightened duplicity—and, after all, not everyone can be an actor, nor wants to be—he can safely forget about practicing gamesmanship because there's no absolute need for it.

The real danger for the gamer comes when the intended victim is awake to what's going on, at which point the gamer may find himself having to deal with the embarrassment and humiliation of being found out.

What every golfer does need though, is an antidote to other people's gamesmanship.

The Antidote

Essentially the antidote comprises an understanding of the fact that, if the gamer is allowed to add his spin to the information being fed into the intended victim's subconscious, the gamer's succeeded. The primary defense, therefore, is simply to consciously exclude any influence or data that does not materially assist the subconscious to formulate and execute the shot. Nothing must be allowed to enter the subconscious that might undermine the expectation of success it has developed through goal-setting, visualization and affirmation.

Despite all these practiced defenses, the gamer may well disrupt his target's concentration by, say, making a noise at the top of his backswing. At that point the only thing to do is bail out of the shot. Step back from the ball and start the entire pre-shot routine—the successive visualizations, the switching off of conscious thought—all over again. Above all don't be hurried. If an expectant glance at the source of the interruption draws an apology, so much the better. If the gamer survives the embarrassment of being fingered by his target, he'll quickly tire of such tricks if they merely result in the intended victim taking so much longer to play his stroke.

A more proactive strategy to combat gamesmanship is to perceive every action of the gaming opponent as a component of his wider game: every little trick he pulls reveals something about him that is grist to the mill of the straight player's awareness. If the straight player's not sure if his opponent is pulling gaming tricks, he simply suspends his judgment on it. He doesn't say to himself, "This character's trying to psyche me out. How do I handle it?" He just remains aware of what the opponent is doing and refuses to be lured into making judgments about him or his antics. And he remembers that, whatever his opponent does, the only way he can win in the end is by playing better golf.

It's that suspension of judgment—the refusal to get annoyed—that's the key. Value judgments, expressed as anger or frustration, not only confuse the subconscious but give encouragement to the gamer. It's not necessary to develop an arsenal of gamesmanship ploys as a defense against gamers. If the gamer's messages can be received non-judgmentally as items of information about his game, there's no need to try to send back messages in response: such messages will reach the gamer of their own accord.

And 999 times out of 1000, they'll be enough to thwart him.

If, after trying the defensive exercises outlined here, the golfer still finds himself a sucker for a good gamer, he should go out of his way to watch the best of them at work. The good gamers are seldom difficult to identify, because they tend to develop reputations. Some gamers indulge in gamesmanship precisely because they hunger for the gamer's reputation for being hard-bitten—and where that's the case, all they're really doing is trying to mask their underlying vulnerability, their underlying lack of confidence in themselves and their golfing skills.

Seeking the accomplished gamers out, and analyzing the way they feed damaging information or perceptions into the opponent's subconscious, will arm even the most susceptible golfer against their tricks.

15

Five Hot Tips for the Handicap Player

It is nothing new or original to say that golf is played one stroke at a time, but it took me years to realize it.

—Bobby Jones

All my advice to the golfer in the chapters leading up to this one has been centered around mental preparation—how to train the computerlike human brain to express the individual's true and full golfing potential. That's an aspect of the game that I feel has been somewhat neglected by golfing writers, though it's at least as important as the physical aspects like swing planes, grip, follow-through and club selection.

Golf is, in the end, a mind game.

I'm a decent player myself, but I generally shrink from offering advice on golfing technique. I'm a professional caddy, not a professional golfer, and I feel there are plenty of instructional books out there— including excellent ones by Greg Norman and Tiger Woods—dealing with the physical mechanics of the game. But for all that, I haven't spent 25 years on the world's professional golf circuits without learning a trick or two that the handicap golfer can use to knock a few strokes off his score.

Not all of my time is spent around the world's best professional golfers. I also have commitments to promising young beginners in New Zealand through my own organization, the Steve Williams Foundation, which, like my boss's Tiger Woods Foundation, is aimed at creating golf opportunities for underprivileged youth. Also, as roving ambassador for the Clearwater Golf Resort in Christchurch, New Zealand, I have a stake in helping any amateur player on a handicap.

Golf's for everyone, and the more people who gain satisfaction from constant improvement, the better it is for the game.

Though I don't swing a club very often these days—being around Tiger so much of the time makes me feel my own game is inadequate—I'm in a unique position to analyze the main limitations that handicap players put on themselves.

With all this in mind, here are my five hot tips for the handicap player.

Take More Club

The biggest problem I see among amateur golfers is they don't take enough club. The key to good golf is hitting the ball pin-high, but there's a strong tendency among amateur golfers to not play within themselves. Part of the problem is that they sit down to watch golf on TV and they see the professionals select an eight iron for, say, a 160-yard shot. Sure, that's an eight iron for Tiger Woods or Ernie Els or Phil Mickelson, but for an amateur player it's more like a six or a seven.

Another element to the problem is the widespread practice of amateurs putting 100 percent effort into each shot. You've got to play within yourself. Too many amateur players swing way too hard. Often there's a bit of ego in it—the desire to show how far they can make the ball go with a particular club. But that's counterproductive, firstly because going for the maximum distance ensures you're going to spray it around a lot more, and secondly because it's tiring. People mostly don't think of golf in terms of the need for stamina, but after you've been out on the course a few hours belting away as hard as you can, you can't help but get tired, and you lose accuracy and consistency as a result. There's only one thing in golf that counts, and that's the score at the end of the day. How far you hit the ball each time is irrelevant; it's how often you have to hit it that counts.

I was able to demonstrate the tendency for amateurs to take too little club when I hosted a round for 132 invited amateurs at my roving ambassadorial club of Clearwater in 2001. My job was to stand on the tee of a 164-yard par three hole, welcome each group as it came through, and offer the caddy's advice on how best to play the hole.

The shot was into the wind, and I'd tell them how far it was and most of them would say, "That's a five or a six iron." I thought to myself,

"Tiger would be hitting a six iron on this hole, but most of these players shouldn't be."

The results proved me right. Of those 132 players, by far the majority of whom played a five or a six iron, only four actually managed to get the ball past the pin.

And it wasn't for lack of effort.

As I pointed out in an earlier chapter, Tiger and the professionals play at about 75 percent of their physical capacity most of the time. On certain shots when the circumstances are favorable, Tiger may reach out with an 85 percent effort, but only at clinics and demonstrations will he stretch his effort above 90 percent.

To find out whether they're taking enough club, I suggest handicap players take an extra scorecard with them. They should write down the club they used on each approach shot, and mark the shot with "S" if it's short, "L" if it's long and "P" if it's pin-high.

Then the next day go out on the same course and play one club extra—that is, say, a five iron where before you would have played a six—and I guarantee you end up with more P's than you had S's the previous day.

Take one club more and you'll be amazed how much better you score.

Improve Your Feel

Golf is a game of feel, and to improve this aspect of the game I recommend using a drill I've seen Tiger employ time and again.

On the driving range he'll choose a flag that could be at any distance between 120 and 150 yards. Then he'll hit every club in the bag to that same flag. His three iron, for example, would normally go 215 yards, but now he's trying to hit it just 120 yards. There's no better exercise that I know of for developing feel. It's also a great way of being able to instruct your subconscious on how you have to swing any club to make the ball go a particular distance.

In this exercise, the bigger the club the more controlled the swing has to be to get it close to the target. It's thus a great exercise for countering the tendency to want to hit the ball as hard as possible every time.

When you know how far you can hit every club, then you're playing within yourself and you're playing with feel.

Play to Your Strengths and Away from Your Weaknesses

You've got to start out in the game with good fundamentals: make sure you've got a decent grip and a good stance, and you know how far you can go with each club while still playing within yourself. But to make a sudden improvement in your score without spending hours on the practice range, set about learning how to play the course in a way that recognizes your strengths and avoids your weaknesses.

If you get on a hole with a dogleg to the left, and like most amateurs you're a chronic slicer of the ball, find out what club you need to hit the safest distance on that particular hole. Go round the course and work out the best way of playing it without making mistakes. When you're a handicap golfer it's not the greatest number of good shots that counts, but the least number of bad ones. Set out to play a trouble-free round and your score's got to come down.

To this end I recommend keeping a set of notes on each course.

Jot down the things to look out for and the things to avoid, and this is where you'll save yourself strokes. If there's a bunker at your home club that you regularly get into off the tee, find out the distance to it and play the club that will keep you short of it.

To improve quickly without putting any extra time into your game you need to get the most out of it that you can. You have to take your game the way it is and maximize it.

Remember, golf is all about how often you hit the ball, not how far you hit it.

Play Every Shot in Isolation

If there's a single theme to my approach to the mind game of golf, it's that every shot has to be played as if it was the only one of the day. That means creating that exclusive cocoon for yourself in both time and space, where everything that occurred beforehand and everything that may follow is excluded from the execution of this particular shot. This isn't computer-age science: the quote at the head of this chapter from the great Bobby Jones (U.S. Open winner 1923, 1926, 1929, 1930; British Open winner 1926, 1927 and 1930—all while still an amateur) bears that out.

But there really is no other way to play the game. You've got to take the view that you only have one chance in golf, and that rests with the next shot. Good or bad, the previous shot, the previous hole, is already down on the scorecard. There's nothing you can do about it now. It's as irrelevant as last week's news.

Same goes for the shot to follow the immediate one: you don't even know what that shot is going to be until you execute the present one, so there's no point in considering it or worrying about it until you get to it.

The trick is to play in the now—not in the past and not in the future.

Keep Up with the Technology

Golf equipment has come a long way since the days of wooden-shafted clubs, and balls stuffed with feathers.

Technology never sleeps.

Like everything else in life, the technological side of golf has evolved, and continues to evolve. The equipment available now is vastly superior to what it was a few years ago, and it continues to improve in terms of both clubs and balls. If you want to get the most out of your game, you've got to take advantage of advances in technology.

There's a wide choice of balls available now, and they all have different flight characteristics. Cover patterns differ, and these affect both the distance and the trajectory that the ball takes in flight. Because consistency is so vital in golf, it's important that you stick to the same golf ball all the time. You can't be consistent if you're using one ball one week and a different one the next. Find a ball that you like, one that you feel comfortable with and that responds consistently to the way you play. Then stick with it.

With clubs, it's important to get a set that suits the player, and for that you need the advice of a golf pro.

Too many players these days are buying their clubs at department stores. There may be nothing wrong with the clubs themselves, they may be well made by a respected manufacturer, but the staff at the department store usually aren't qualified to tell you which set suits you and your handicap range. Go to a golf pro and explain how you play the game and what you're hoping to get out of your purchase. A pro at the golf club or driving range is going to know what's best for your game.

Try out the new metal-wood drivers with the big heads and the graphite shafts. Try the cavity-back irons. Get the wedges that can help you get out of difficult spots. Get the putter that's right for you—there are lots of different putters around these days, all based on new ideas of how to line up and roll the ball better.

If you want to maximize your game, spend a bit of money on the equipment that's best for you, and go from there.

16

Caddying in the Zone

If your caddy coaches you on the tee, "Hit it down the left with a little draw," ignore him. All you do on the tee is try not to hit the caddy.
— Jim Murray (Sportswriter 1919–98).

My career has been that of a man on a mission: to reinvent the role of the caddy. Peter Thomson was my inspiration, and the 1976 New Zealand Open at Heretaunga was my road to Damascus. Ever since, I've been fixated by the idea that the caddy should offer the professional golfer as vital a service as the mechanic offers the racing driver. With all three of my main employers—Norman, Floyd and Woods—I have striven to develop a partnership that comes as close to that model as possible. With Tiger Woods in particular I believe we've approached the golfer–caddy relationship with a level of excellence and success unprecedented in the game.

When Peter Thomson first planted the germ of this ambition in my mind, it was a radical idea indeed. Even 30 years ago the role of caddy was still tainted by perceptions hanging over from the early days of the Scottish game.

The word itself is believed to derive from the French *cadet*, and to have been taken across the English Channel by the ill-fated Mary Queen of Scots. Born and educated in France, she had her fellow students—*mes cadets*—carry her clubs for her when she played there, and the term stuck after she moved to Scotland in 1561. There it became synonymous with the seamen and shepherds who, while not otherwise gainfully employed, hefted bundles of wooden-shafted clubs round coastal links for the wealthy, leisured personages who were then the principal patrons of the game.

In those days caddies were less likely to be paid in cash than in consumables, usually of the alcoholic variety, which gave rise to their reputation for drunkenness and licentiousness. Horace Hutchinson (1859–1932), the author of the first anthology of the game (*Golf*, The Badminton Library, 1890), went so far as to describe the caddy in 1900 as "a reckless, feckless creature," and to warn players against paying them too much in cash in case they squandered it on strong drink.

On the gut-wrenching Carnoustie course in Scotland, where the game has been played since 1560, and which has hosted half a dozen British Opens since 1931, the 452-yard par-four 10th hole remains a monument to the old-style caddy's inveterate inebriation. It's called "South America" after an erstwhile looper's loudly proclaimed late-night ambition to abscond to that far continent to seek his fortune. He duly set off, but only got as far as the 10th tee, where he was found the next morning sleeping off his previous night's resolve.

Despite the fabled indiscretions of many of the early caddies, over time the value of one who knew both the course, and the best strategic uses of the clubs he was carrying, came to be recognized as an indispensable aid to the serious golfer. That led to the caddy developing today's complex professional persona combining the roles of butler, psychologist and mathematician. The venerable *Times* of London encapsulated this expanded role in its description of the modern caddy as someone who "must be utterly reliable, loyal and scientifically precise," qualities that required "a little of Jeeves; a little of Will Summers (the fool who alone dared tell Henry VIII the truth); a little of Pythagoras."

I believe I embody that definition.

Putting the Bite Back in Tiger

The 1998 season hadn't been a good one for Tiger Woods. The euphoria of his record-breaking 12-stroke Masters triumph the previous year had all but dissipated. He'd managed only one win on the PGA Tour, the BellSouth Classic, though he'd thrilled his mother, Kultida, by taking out the international Johnnie Walker Classic in her home country of Thailand. The magic of '97, though, seemed to have deserted him, and that awesome performance at Augusta was beginning to look like a flash in the pan.

That was the point at which he teamed up with me.

We had a nodding acquaintance from the times Tiger had played against Greg Norman and Raymond Floyd. Tiger was friendly with both of my previous long-term bosses. He later said that many of Norman's greatest successes had been achieved with my help, and that getting me on his bag had brought about change to Floyd's ailing career.

The disappointing 1998 season, lightened only by the BellSouth and Thai victories, had seemed to accentuate Tiger's need for a caddy better attuned to the confident young pro he had become.

Fluff Cowan had done a great job of shepherding the youngster through the mental minefield of his switch from the amateur to the professional ranks, but the 1997 Masters triumph had demonstrated emphatically that that transition period was now behind him. Tiger no longer needed a caddy to look after him. He needed a caddy to stimulate him.

It took a while for our new partnership to gel, because there were big changes in it for both of us. For Tiger it was a case of switching his game plan from defense to attack, while for me it was adjusting to working for the first time for a man younger than myself.

But after that breakthrough moment in our relationship on the 15th hole in the first round of the 1999 Hilton Head Classic at South Carolina's Harbour Town Golf Club, there could be no doubt about our eventual success. By the end of that season, we had set a PGA Tour earnings record of $6.6 million, double the total of the nearest competitor, David Duval.

We won eight tournaments that year, the first time such a feat had been accomplished since Johnny Miller pulled it off in 1974. Four of those wins were on the trot, something not achieved since Ben Hogan did it in 1953. The most important was the PGA at Medinah which, along with the '97 Masters, made Tiger, at 24, the youngest double-major winner since Seve Ballesteros. (Though also 24 when he won his second major, Ballesteros was actually nine months younger than Tiger when he made the double.)

We achieved even greater things in 2000 and 2001 —the likes of which had never been seen in the game over so short a time frame. There were the nine Tour victories of 2000 for a new single-season record earnings total of $9.1 million, the most wins in a season since Sam Snead's 11 in 1950. Most startling, though, were the three consecutive major titles—the British and U.S. Opens and the PGA—which, along with Tiger's '97 Masters title, gave him a career Grand Slam. That put him in the same exclusive company as Gene Sarazen, Ben Hogan, Jack Nicklaus and Gary Player. And of those four greats, only Hogan had managed to win three majors in a single season.

The U.S. Open victory was particularly historic because Tiger's 15-stroke winning margin was a record for a major. The previous holder was no less ancient and historic a figure than Old Tom Morris, who trounced the field by 13 strokes in winning the third of his four British opens way back in 1864, at a time when Britain's Queen Victoria was less than halfway through her 64-year reign.

Five more victories followed in 2001, the highlight being Tiger's second Masters title. Coming on top of his winning the three other majors the previous year, it meant he became the first player in the history of the game to hold all four titles at once. Technically it wasn't a true Grand Slam because the titles hadn't all been won in the same year, but it was as close as anyone has ever gotten to it.

The Caddy as Butler

So what is it about my caddying that can help to reignite careers that otherwise look as if they're in the doldrums?

My career began at a time when the emerging craft of caddying was coming face to face with new technology in the form of the electric or petrol-driven golf cart. Just before my life-altering encounter with Peter Thomson, British golfing great Sir (Thomas) Henry Cotton confidently predicted that golf carts would spell the demise of the caddy.

"The caddy is still part of the golf scene," Cotton (British Open champion 1934, 1937 and 1948) wrote in 1975, "but his end is in sight as costs rise and the mechanized buggy takes over his purely physical purpose. Only in professional tournaments, where caddies' costs are deductible tax expenses, are they still common, and even then many are but callow youths with little experience of the course."

Time proved Cotton partly right about golf carts, but other career loopers and I have made nonsense of his perception of professional caddies as "callow youths." The mechanized golf cart did indeed spell the demise of beast-of-burden amateur caddies—at least on courses where carts became compulsory to speed up playing times—and whose only previous responsibilities to their clients had been to show up, keep up and shut up.

But carts also served to differentiate between the amateur and the professional caddy in more ways than just the tax advantages. As I learned from Thomson, the caddy could take over a range of tactical, strategic and organizational chores—things we today lump under the catch-all term of "course management"—leaving the golfer to concentrate on making the shots. Compared to that, the purely physical task of carting a bag of clubs round the course is now only a relatively minor part of the caddy's role as butler, despite its high profile in these days of multi-camera television coverage. Away from the cameras, the caddy-as-butler looks after everything from the provision of snacks, drinks and wet-weather gear, to maintaining the clubs and ensuring there are no more than the regulation 14 in the bag. From umbrella-holder to crowd-controller, he's the epitome of the modern-day Jeeves.

The Caddy as Psychologist

The caddy-as-psychologist is primarily concerned with minimizing, as far as possible, the psychological negatives that are the inevitable by-product of the game. He maintains at all times a calming and reassuring influence and, between shots, gives the golfer the mental respite of conversation about anything but golf.

From time to time the caddy's psychological role is even extended to coaching. Perhaps the most startling such incident in my career came when I was on temporary loan from Raymond Floyd to Mike Clayton, an Australian playing—badly—in the final round of the 1990 Scottish Open. Though accurate enough off the tee and with his approach shots, Clayton's putting was destroying his game. With five holes to play, I had had enough.

"I'm fed up watching you putt," I told Clayton. "You're awful."

Then I gave him an impromptu putting lesson based on Greg Norman's practice of lining it up with his right hand first. Clayton went on to birdie three of the remaining holes. In a practice round at Scotscraig the following day, Clayton needed only 26 putts on his way to setting a new course record of 63, including seven birdies and an eagle.

Also within the ambit of psychologist is the insulation the caddy provides the golfer against the inevitable intrusions of the media. While I have a well-earned reputation for discouraging journalists from prying too avidly into my bosses' private lives, as distinct from their public ones, I point to my colleague and good friend Fanny Sunesson as the soul of discretion among caddies. Sunesson, a Swede, has caddied for Nick Faldo since 1990, during which time her boss survived two marriage breakups that had the media slavering for the juicy details. But at no stage could Sunesson be drawn by the media into revealing anything of this side of her boss' life. Her discretion has been the rock that anchored Nick Faldo's professional career, even as his personal life went through a period of turbulence.

The core contribution of the modern professional caddy as psychologist lies, however, in allowing the client to approach the game with only one consideration in mind: the next shot. Good caddies take care of the big picture, the strategic approach to the hole, to the course and to the tournament. The overall approach is worked out with the player beforehand, but once play is under way it's the caddy who ensures they stick to the game plan, while the golfer concentrates on the only thing that counts: that next shot.

In my case that doesn't always extend to putting. Once the ball's on the green, I generally leave the reading of the putt to my client. I might say which way the putt will break, but putting's all about speed and feel, and I leave the rest to the golfer.

The Caddy as Mathematician

The expansion of the role of the caddy during my career began with the provision of yardages, the distances to the hole from the tee or from any point on the fairway. In my early days I produced these for my clients by personally walking the course as often as three times before each tournament. I thereby developed so measured a stride that, when in later years laser-measuring devices came on the market, I would use them only to confirm my calculations, rather than the other way round. Though accurate yardage charts are now freely available on most major Tour courses, I still prefer to pace out holes I'm not familiar with, rather than resort to the laser.

Providing yardages, along with such advice as wind strength and direction, may be the main role of the caddy as mathematician, but it's not the only one. As well as things like double-checking scores, the caddy has to be on the lookout for potential rule breaches by his client. For example, early in my career I intervened when Greg Norman was about to saddle himself with two penalty shots on the 15th green in the final round of the 1983 New South Wales Open in Australia. Norman was in a head-to-head battle with fellow Australian David Graham, and had marked his ball, then moved the marker back the regulation putter-width to clear the way for Graham. But when he himself came to putt, Norman forgot to take his marker back the putter-width. I pointed out the oversight, thereby preventing a two-shot penalty. Norman went on to win the tournament.

Quantifying the Contribution

It's difficult to measure empirically a caddy's contribution to the player's success. After all, it's the player whose performance ultimately decides the outcome of any game or tournament, no matter how useful the caddy's input.

That said, some indication of my worth as Tiger's caddy can be gained by comparing his statistics for his first two years on the PGA Tour (1997 and 1998), before we teamed up, with his subsequent five (up to the end of 2003). Such a comparison can only be indicative rather than empirical because there are so many variables that the raw statistics don't take into account. That's especially so in Tiger's case, given that those first two years comprised his transition from amateur to profes-sional; after that he could be expected to improve regardless of who he had caddying for him. But by the same token, that transitional period included his unparalleled triumph in the 1997 Masters, which stands out as a dramatic spike on his performance graph, the more so because of the long run of flat performances that followed. Also, the statistical validity of the comparison—such as it is—is strengthened by the second compar-ative period (1999–2003 inclusive) being more than double the length of the first.

In both 1997 and 1998 Tiger was second on the PGA's average scoring list with, respectively, 69.1 (behind Nick Price on 68.98) and

69.21 (behind David Duval on 69.13). That gave him an average over those two years of 69.155 strokes per round.

But when I joined up with him he had the best scoring average on the Tour for every one of the next five years: 68.43 in 1999 (ahead of Duval on 69.17), 67.79 in 2000 (ahead of Phil Mickelson on 69.25), 68.81 in 2001 (ahead of Davis Love III on 69.06), 68.56 in 2002 (ahead of Vijay Singh on 69.47) and 68.41 in 2003 (again ahead of Singh on 68.65). That gave Tiger a five-year average of 68.4, an improvement of 0.755 strokes per round over his previous two-year average.

In other words, Tiger's five-year average in that period was more than three-quarters of a stroke better per round—that is, over three strokes per tournament—than his two-year average was before.

Again, one can only speculate how much of that improvement is directly attributable to the caddy's influence, but such is the intensity of the competition on the PGA Tour that three strokes per tournament is usually enough to turn a top-five finish into an outright victory.

Tiger, however, is confident in the value of my contribution to his rising success rate. "Stevie can just read me, to the point when he knows when to say something and when not to say something," Tiger said after our British Open win in 2000.

He was even more complimentary about my input when they won the PGA the same year. "Without Stevie, I wouldn't have won," he said, going on to explain why I had taken the extraordinary step of interrupting him just as he was about to play an iron shot on Valhalla's 12th. "The wind had changed suddenly and he told me to hit it harder than we had planned. He had the guts to do that, and I listened because I respect him so much."

Surviving the Stresses

That respect survived an incident at the 2003 Masters, when I was widely criticized for persuading Tiger to change the way he played the short par-four 350-yard third hole at Augusta.

Tiger was in contention for a record third Masters title in a row when I talked him out of teeing off conservatively with a two iron, instead suggesting the aggressive option of using a driver. My idea was for Tiger to drive it onto the up-slope close to the green, giving him an easy pitch to a difficult pin position, and thereby a great chance for a birdie that would close the gap on the eventual winner, Mike Weir. Tiger took my advice, but the drive flew into the trees. The only way out, other than an even more costly drop, was a left-handed shot back onto the fairway. Tiger ended up double-bogeying the hole, and it was that drive off the tee, more than any other shot, that ruined his chances of catching Weir.

Tiger was certainly upset at the outcome of the shot but, far from firing me as the media anticipated, he took the blame for the result on himself.

"I made a mental blunder," he said afterwards. "It was a bad decision."

Conspirators at the President's Cup

However you want to measure my contribution as butler, psychologist and mathematician to Tiger Woods, the by-product of our professional association has been an extraordinarily strong and mutually respectful personal relationship. This became apparent to the world at large in January of 2002 when Tiger, at my invitation, made his first professional visit to the South Pacific to compete in the New Zealand Open, at my old home course of Paraparaumu. To a country that has more golf courses per head of population than any other (400 for 4 million people, or one for every 10,000), Tiger's visit was an enormous fillip to the game in New Zealand.

The tournament itself was won by the Australian veteran Craig Parry, possibly in part because Tiger took a rare Saturday night off to watch me drive my Caddyshack V8 at the Palmerston North International Speedway. He then delighted the crowd by lapping the circuit on the back of the race marshall's truck.

Tiger received appearance money for taking part in the New Zealand Open but, relative to the huge events on the PGA circuit, it would normally have been too low-paying a tournament to justify his traveling to such a remote outpost of the game.

He did it for me.

The closeness of our relationship was even more graphically illustrated towards the end of 2003, when both of us were contemplating the same radical change to their personal circumstances.

I had taken the advantage of a break in Tiger's playing schedule to dash home to New Zealand for a few days before we met up again to play the President's Cup in South Africa. I was home just long enough to take the Caddyshack Mustang south from its Auckland home to the dirt-track racing circuit at Kihikihi in rural Waikato. As usual, I was accompanied on the trip by my long-time girlfriend, Kirsty Miller.

Almost hidden behind the wall of my media-shyness, Kirsty, 28, has been my near-constant companion since we met at a charity golf tournament in 1998 in Waikanae, New Zealand. Kirsty is a golfer who shares my family and emotional ties to the two local links: her father, Ian Miller, is a former captain of the nearby Waikanae Golf Club, where I often played as a junior. Ian Miller knew me well before I set out on my lifetime quest to become one of golf's most successful caddies. Because of both her father's and her partner's long associations with the game, Kirsty was as thrilled as any local at Tiger's decision to play the New Zealand Open at Paraparaumu in 2002.

For four years Kirsty had traveled with me around the PGA Tour circuit, becoming a close friend of Tiger and his parents, Kultida and Earl. A former foreign-exchange broker, she acted in between times as chief executive to the Steve Williams Foundation, set up to nurture young golfers.

So golf had become as much a part of Kirsty's way of life as it had mine when, on November 16, 2003, I gunned the Caddyshack Mustang out of the pits onto the Kihikihi track. As I set out on my warm-up lap, I unfurled a banner along the side of the car and it fluttered there throughout my first circuit of the track. In huge lettering the banner read, "Happy birthday, Kirsty."

But that wasn't all.

In equally strident characters it popped the eternal question, "Will you marry me?"

I was strapped into the car and couldn't see much. I signaled thumbs-up or thumbs-down to Kirsty as I passed her in the stand with the banner flapping in my slipstream. She hesitated only as long as it took for the proposal to sink in. Then she gave me the thumbs-up in return.

After the race I did the formal and traditional thing: I got the ring out and got down on my knee. Kirsty hadn't changed her mind between the warm-up and the victory lap.

Rednecks and Sunsets

A week later, at the President's Cup in George, South Africa, I entertained Tiger with the story of my successful marriage proposal, with particular emphasis on the banner on the Mustang and the bended knee afterwards.

Tiger was highly amused. "I always thought you were a redneck," he told me. "Now I know for sure."

Immediately after the President's Cup (which resulted in an unprecedented 17–17 draw between the International and American teams), it was my turn to chuckle as Tiger set about upholding his end of a pact we'd agreed to weeks earlier.

It was a beautiful evening on the Shamwari Game Reserve, near Port Elizabeth, as Tiger strolled through the African bush a couple of days later with his Swedish girlfriend of two years, Elin Nordegren. They'd met through Ryder Cup player and five-times PGA Tour winner Jesper Parnevik. Jesper and his wife, Mia, had hired Elin, a part-time model, as nanny to their four kids (the youngest of whom is named Phoenix in memory of Jesper's first PGA Tour victory, the Phoenix Open of 1998). Elin, 23, is the daughter of Sweden's Immigration Minister, Barbro Holmberg, and Thomas Nordegren, a Washington-based correspondent for Swedish Radio.

A week after I made my flamboyant proposal to Kirsty Miller, Tiger Woods went down on one knee before the equally unsuspecting Elin in the deafening stillness of the African sunset.

"To putt for victory in a major is nothing in comparison," Tiger would later say of his popping the question to Elin. "It was a thriller. Even if you say 'Will you marry me?' with the right feeling, the answer could be 'No.'" But like a putt with the right feel, Tiger's proposal got the same response from Elin that mine had gotten from Kirsty.

Back at the game reserve, Kirsty and I joined Tiger's long-time friend Jerry Chang and his wife, Danielle, in congratulating them.

We had a little bit of a plan between the two of us. I got engaged on Kirsty's birthday, then Tiger did it a week later. The girls were a bit annoyed about that, but Tiger wouldn't do it unless I did it. That's how close the friendship is.

Much water has passed under the bridge since then. A few months after the marriage proposals, Tiger and Elin wed, and in October 2005, Kirsty and I had a baby son whom we've named Jett Baillie.

While our personal lives took a new direction as we both formalized our relationships with our life partners, there was no faltering in the pace of our professional activities.

The 2004 season was a poor one for us by Tiger's usual extraordinary standards: no majors and just a single Tour win in America. Of course, the media—or the more superficial of them—trumpeted Tiger's relative lack of success that year as evidence that he was washed up. This was despite his candor in explaining that the dip in his form was brought about by the major modifications he was making to his swing, to get yet more distance out of it.

The smarter media commentators, however, analyzed Tiger's performance and realized that his short game was as deadly as ever—it was only his drives off the tee that were letting him down, skewing off into the rough and the trees.

It took Tiger all that year to get his revised swing right, but by December he had it under control. From the four tournaments he played through into 2005, he scored three wins and a second. Those wins were just the curtain-raiser for another vintage year in 2005, when he won the Masters and the British Open, and finished second to my countryman Michael Campbell in the U.S. Open.

Of course, I had pretty mixed feelings about Campbell's win: it was marvelous to see a fellow Kiwi take out one of the world's greatest sporting titles, but I just wish he hadn't had to beat Tiger to do it.

But that's golf.

And, like life, the game is essentially unchanging, eternal—a game that must be played over and over in the mind before it can be acted out with any realistic expectation of success on the course.

And if there's any occupation in the world, professional or part-time, that demonstrates the ultimate supremacy of mind over matter, golf is it.

Index

Acute pain, defined, 148. *See also* Pain

Aerobic breathing, 114

Aerobic running, 114, 115

Affirmations, 90–98, 102; and relaxation, 112; and visualization, 103; writing, 96–97

Ali, Muhammad, 97

Alliss, Peter, 64

Alpha brain-waves, 116, 119

Anchoring techniques, 122–26, 148

Armour, Tommy, 146–47, 148

Autogenic training, 119–20

Awareness, practicing, 26, 27–28, 29

Azinger, Paul, 127

Baker-Finch, Ian, 55–57, 58, 64

Ballesteros, Severiano, 168; gamesmanship, 153; relaxation techniques, 110

Balls, 164; dimensions, 22; and visualization, 49

Bannister, Roger, 38–39

Bean, Andy, 99–100

Beem, Rich, 131, 135

Beta brain-waves, 116

Bolt, "Terrible" Tommy, 121–22, 128, 133

Brain, and learning, 53

Brain/computer comparison, 21–27, 29, 33–34, 36–38, 39–41

Brain-wave control, 116–20

Breathing, 113–16, 146

Breathing meditation, 117–18

"Butterflies," 45, 48, 51, 145, 149

Caddying, 14, 166–77; history, 166–67, 169–70

Campbell, Michael, 177

Chitengwa, Lewis, 67

Choice, 34–35. *See also* Imagination

Choking, 46–48

Chronic pain, defined, 148. *See also* Pain

Clayton, Mike, 170

Clubs and club selection, 161–62, 164–65

Coles, Neil, 155

Computer/brain comparison, 21–27, 29, 33–34, 36–38, 39–41

Concentration, 42–51, 63–64, 111; and desire, 64; switching off, 50–51

Conscious mind, switching off, 27–29
Cotton, Sir (Thomas) Henry, 169
Coué, Émile, 94
Cowan, Mike "Fluff," 10, 42, 168

Deadlines, as guidelines, 81
Deep breathing, 113–16, 146
Desire, 58–60, 62–71
Desperation, 64
Diaphragm breathing, 113, 146
Distractions. *See* Concentration

Els, Ernie "The Big Easy," 132;
     temperament, 43, 129
Equipment, 164–65
Expectation index, 139–42
Expectation of success, 137–42

Failure, 133
Faldo, Nick, 46, 47, 100, 171;
     mechanical approach, 127, 128
Fear of failure, 144–46
"Feel," 126–28; developing, 162
Fight-or-flight mechanism, 34–35,
     41, 45
Fitzgerald, Peter "Irish," 17
Floyd, Raymond, 9–10, 16, 168;
     concentration, 50; goal-setting,
     77; injuries, 143; visualization,
     99–101
Focusing. *See* Concentration
Form slumps, 52, 54
Four-minute mile, 38–39
Free will, 60
Freud, Sigmund, 22, 28

Gamesmanship, 153–59
Garcia, Sergio, 128
Goal-setting, 62–63, 69–74, 75–89;
     exercise, 71–74; golden rules,

76–79; intermediate goals,
     79–81; short-term goals, 83–89
Goals, written, 70–74, 76
Golf carts, 169–70
Graham, David, 172

Handicap, 39, 79
Handicap players: and desire, 63, 69;
     tips, 160–65
Harmon, Claude "Butch," 10
Harwood, Mike, 56
High handicap players. *See*
     Handicap players
Hutchinson, Horace, 167
Hypnosis, 117

Imagination, 34–41, 52–53, 54–55;
     and snowball effect, 57–58; and
     visualization, 101–102, 104
"In the zone" concept, 18–19, 33.
     See also Peak experience
     concept
Injuries, 143–44. *See also* Pain
Irwin, Hale, 13

Jacklin, Tony, 155
Jones, Bobby, 163

Kasparov, Garry, 101–102

Langer, Bernhard, 147
Leadbetter, David, 127
Leahy, Frank, 96–97
The lie [of the ball], 27
Lydiard, Arthur, 114–15
Lyle, Sandy, 47

Mackay, Roger, 55
Master plan, 79–83; example, 82
Meditation, 117–19

Memory, 23–24, 25–27
Miller, Ian, 175
Miller, Kirsty, 175
Mind-training techniques, 18–20;
    and choking, 48
Moods, 122
Muscular control, 113–16

Nicklaus, Jack, 93, 128; and visuali-
    zation, 106
Nordegren, Elin, 176
Norman, Greg, 10, 16, 168, 172; and
    caddy Steve Williams, 16, 99,
    100; "choking," 46–47; concen-
    tration, 50; injuries, 143; relax-
    ation techniques, 110; switching
    off conscious mind, 28; and
    visualization, 107

Oxygen debt, 114
Ozaki, Masashi "Jumbo," 100

Pain, 143–44, 148–52
Pain management, 149–52
Palmer, Arnold, 56; "choking," 46
Paraparaumu Golf Club, 12
Parnevik, Jesper, 176
Parry, Craig, 55, 174
Peak experience concept, 131–42;
    components, 135–37; and
    expectation, 137–42
Phobias, 35, 47
Physical capacity, percentage used,
    25, 126, 162
Player, Gary, 93
Practice, 24–25
Pre-shot routine, 48–50, 110, 115
Putting, and visualization, 108–109

Ranger Rick syndrome, 39–41
Relaxation, 112; and pain, 150–51
Relaxation techniques, 110–20
"RICE" formula, 150
Roberts, Loren, 144
Rugby, 12, 111, 129–30
Russell, Alex, 12

Self-belief, 105
Self-confidence, 44–46
Senses: and shot-making cycle,
    48–49; and visualization, 103
Shot-making cycle, 48–50; and
    visualization, 49, 106–108
Snead, Sam, 112
Snowball effect, 52–61
Sports psychologists, 33–34
Stadler, Craig, 101
Steve Williams Foundation, 160, 175
Subconscious, 29, 33–34, 37–38,
    40–41, 133, 134, 138; and affir-
    mations, 90–98; and fear of fail-
    ure, 145; and gamesmanship,
    155; and goal-setting, 70; and
    imagination, 38–39; and moods,
    122; and pain, 150; and self-
    confidence, 44; and snowball
    effect, 57–58
Sunesson, Fanny, 171
Swing, 24–25. *See also* Clubs and
    club selection; Shot-making
    cycle

Tall poppy syndrome, 93
Temperament, 128–30
Thomson, Peter, 11, 59, 166; and
    caddy Steve Williams, 13–14,
    15–16
Tips, for handicap players, 160–65

Toledo, Esteban, 131
Toms, David, 132
Tournaments, 39; importance, 79
Training schedules, 86–89
Transcendental meditation (TM),
    118–19
Trevino, Lee, 93; and "feel," 128;
    gamesmanship, 155, 156
Triggers, 125, 148
"Try harder" concept, 133

Value judgments, 29–31
Visualization, 49, 146, 147–48; and
    pain, 151–52; and relaxation,
    112

"The waggles," 146–48
Waite, Grant, 132
Walker, John, 38
Weight training, 115
Weir, Mike, 174
Williams, John, 12–13
Williams, Steve: caddying behavior
    and technique, 42–43, 50,
    166–67, 171–72; client list,
    16–17; early years as caddy,
    13–17, 60; foundation, 160,
    175; hundredth win, 17;
    injuries, 144; physical fitness

regime, 114, 115; and rugby, 12,
    59, 60, 111; youth, 12–15
Woods, Earl: gamesmanship, 155;
    teaching son, 26–27, 43, 65–66,
    67, 135
Woods, Kultida, 167
Woods, Tiger, 17, 128; and caddy
    Mike Cowan, 10, 168; and
    caddy Steve Williams, 9–11, 17,
    167–69, 172–77; and caddies,
    93; concentration, 42–43, 50;
    desire, 65–68; and "feel," 162;
    fitness regime, 114, 115; games-
    manship, 153, 155; and "in the
    zone" concept, 18–19; injuries,
    143; and peak experience con-
    cept, 131–32, 135; physical
    capacity, percentage used, 162;
    relaxation, 112; relaxation tech-
    niques, 110–11; and sports psy-
    chologists, 33; swing, 104;
    teaching by father, 26–27, 43,
    65–66, 67, 135; temperament,
    129

"The yips," 147, 148

Zigler, Zig, 92–93

Other Ulysses Press Mind/Body Titles

ADRENALINE JUNKIES & SEROTONIN SEEKERS: BALANCE YOUR BRAIN CHEMISTRY TO MAXIMIZE ENERGY, STAMINA, MENTAL SHARPNESS, AND EMOTIONAL WELLBEING

Matt Church, $12.95

This handy little book shows how easy it is to tap into the natural "drug store" in one's body—containing adrenaline, serotonin, cortisol, melatonin, and insulin—and activate internal feel-good chemistry.

FIT IN 15: 15-MINUTE MORNING WORKOUTS THAT BALANCE CARDIO, STRENGTH, AND FLEXIBILITY

Steven Stiefel, $14.95

Fit in 15 details a unique, full-body fitness program that even the busiest person can work into a morning schedule. The fun and flexible "7 days/7 workouts" plan lets readers choose from 35 specially designed 15-minute workouts.

THE GOLFER'S GUIDE TO PILATES: STEP-BY-STEP EXERCISES TO LOWER YOUR SCORE

Monica Clyde, $14.95

Pilates has become the premier training choice for top golfers. Now, *The Golfer's Guide to Pilates* offers an affordable and convenient way for all golfers to gain the benefits of this popular conditioning method.

HOW MEDITATION HEALS: A SCIENTIFIC EXPLANATION

Eric Harrison, $12.95

In straightforward, practical terms, *How Meditation Heals* reveals how and why meditation improves the natural functioning of the human body.

TEACH YOURSELF TO MEDITATE IN 10 SIMPLE LESSONS: DISCOVER RELAXATION AND CLARITY OF MIND IN JUST MINUTES A DAY

Eric Harrison, $12.95

Guides the reader through ten easy-to-follow core meditations. Also included are practical and enjoyable "spot meditations" that require only a few minutes a day and can be incorporated into the busiest of schedules.

ULTIMATE CORE BALL WORKOUT: STRENGTHENING AND SCULPTING EXERCISES WITH OVER 200 STEP-BY-STEP PHOTOS

Jeanine Detz, $14.95

Maximizes today's hottest area of fitness—core training—by tapping the power of the exercise ball with these strengthening and sculpting exercises.

WEIGHTS ON THE BALL WORKBOOK: STEP-BY-STEP GUIDE WITH OVER 350 PHOTOS

Steven Stiefel, $14.95

With exercises suited for all skill levels, *Weights on the Ball Workbook* shows how to simultaneously use weights and the exercise ball for the ultimate total-body workout.

WORKOUTS FROM BOXING'S GREATEST CHAMPS

Gary Todd, $14.95

Features dramatic photos, workout secrets and behind-the-scenes details of Muhammad Ali, Roy Jones, Jr., Fernando Vargas and other legends.

YOGA IN FOCUS: POSTURES, SEQUENCES AND MEDITATIONS

Jessie Chapman   photographs by Dhyan, $14.95

A beautiful celebration of yoga that's both useful for learning the techniques and inspiring in its artistic approach to presenting the body in yoga positions.

To order these books call 800-377-2542 or 510-601-8301, fax 510-601-8307, e-mail ulysses@ulyssespress.com, or write to Ulysses Press, P.O. Box 3440, Berkeley, CA 94703. All retail orders are shipped free of charge. California residents must include sales tax. Allow two to three weeks for delivery.

Acknowledgments

The authors express their appreciation for the invaluable assistance of Dr. David Whitehead of Christchurch Hospital for his advice on medical aspects of this book; John Maber of Hamilton for his review of the draft; and Hamish Ireland of Christchurch for his valued support and encouragement.

About the Authors

Steve Williams is the most successful caddy in the history of golf, with more than 100 tournament wins to his credit. A professional caddy since he was 15 years old, he has circled the globe working with world-class golfers. Steve now caddies for Tiger Woods. When not traveling, you might find him behind the wheel of one of his Caddyshack Racing dirt track Mustang Saloons. He lives in New Zealand with his wife Kirsty and son Jett Baillie. **Hugh de Lacy** is a best-selling author and an award-winning investigative journalist, business/political writer and columnist. He worked on daily newspapers and magazines in New Zealand until going freelance in 1990. In between times he served as Parliamentary press secretary to a Minister of Justice, and took a six-year sabbatical from journalism to work as a sheep-shearer. He operates his freelance writing agency, Catching Pen Associates, from the North Canterbury home he shares with his wife Roche and their son Hugh jun.